'Reading this book feels like having a conversation with a trusted friend – thoughtful, engaging, and reflective. Readers are challenged to revisit and update their narratives around leadership, mindfulness, and emotional intelligence, offering stories and metaphors that make complex ideas accessible. Jess encourages reflection and action, sparking insights for individuals and teams. A book for anyone wanting to pause, grow, and lead with greater intention.'

Hannah Macdougall, *PhD, PLY*

'*Leaders Who Thrive* is a timely and practical guide for modern leadership. This book challenges traditional thinking by placing mindfulness, emotional intelligence, and wellbeing at the centre of effective leadership. It offers a grounded, evidence-based framework that helps leaders better understand themselves, connect with their teams, and lead with clarity and intent. The insights are both accessible and actionable, making it essential reading for emerging leaders and those looking to evolve their leadership approach in today's complex, high-pressure environments.'

Michael Field, *Founding Partner, EvettField Partners*

Leaders Who Thrive

This book integrates theoretical and practical perspectives to equip leaders with tools to thrive in today's complex workplace environments. Combining mindfulness and emotional intelligence, this book provides actionable tools to enhance self-awareness, foster meaningful relationships, and build resilience under pressure.

In an era of increasing burnout and rising expectations for emotional intelligence in leadership, this book equips leaders to meet modern challenges with authenticity, presence, and purpose. It delves into cultivating focus in distraction-heavy lives, managing stress, and creating inclusive cultures that foster psychological safety and connection. Featuring insights from neuroscience, positive psychology, and real-world leadership practices, this book bridges the gap between theory and application. It begins with a discussion of the meaning of leadership in today's world, and an introduction to mindfulness and its real-world applications. Later chapters address self-awareness and empathy before the final chapter brings these concepts together to explain how readers can apply them to any leadership context. This transformative approach enables readers to practice and develop these concepts in real-world settings to mature their own skills to lead with clarity, empathy, and intention.

This is a vital practical resource for any leader, from emerging leaders to HR professionals and seasoned executives alike. Students, particularly those on leadership or business courses, will also benefit from the combination of theory and practice.

Jessica Jasch is the founder of J-Leigh, a wellbeing consulting and coaching service. She has two bachelor's degrees from Queensland University of Technology and has since completed her master's degree in Applied Positive Psychology from the University of Melbourne.

Leaders Who Thrive

A Mindful Antidote to Disconnected Teams

Jessica Jasch

Routledge
Taylor & Francis Group
LONDON AND NEW YORK

Designed Cover: Getty Images

First published 2027
by Routledge
4 Park Square, Milton Park, Abingdon, Oxon OX14 4RN

and by Routledge
605 Third Avenue, New York, NY 10158

Routledge is an imprint of the Taylor & Francis Group, an informa business

British Library Cataloguing-in-Publication Data
A catalogue record for this book is available from the British Library

ISBN: 9781041058977 (hbk)
ISBN: 9781041058953 (pbk)
ISBN: 9781003632771 (ebk)

DOI: 10.4324/9781003632771

Typeset in Galliard
by Deanta Global Publishing Services, Chennai, India

Dedicated to Stormie Lou. To my little schnook – who spent our eight years together being my floofy soulmate, keeping me laughing and emotionally regulated, and teaching me that if you have something to say, you'd better use that voice of yours and howl. I started this book with you, and now you can end the book with me too. I love, and miss, you forever.

Contents

Acknowledgements

I want to begin by thanking Darren for getting this ball rolling – writing a book has forever been a desire of mine, and one simple conversation began the process of actually making it a reality. I also want to thank my publishing team – Andrew, Payal, and Felicia – for helping this first-time author navigate her way through the process, always being responsive when I needed them, but at the same time giving me enough space to simply be in writing mode.

I want to thank my first readers, Hannah and Michael. Thank you for being trustworthy enough for me to share the most vulnerable phase of writing, knowing I would get honest and open feedback, and for enthusiastically doing so despite your own busy businesses and lives. I also want to acknowledge everyone who has in some way informed or inspired my work and my own lessons in leadership, whether intended or not. Just having the opportunity to have the experiences I have had so far has helped to form my understanding of these concepts we explore, and for that I'm grateful.

To my ever-steady cheer team who have only ever celebrated and encouraged me throughout this process and everything else that was happening along with it – that has felt more valuable than I can ever express. Whether it was your belief that this was totally achievable, the real-time encouragement and space (or outright nudges) to just keep writing even when it got hard or life got full, or the reflections that helped me remember just how much progress I've made, it's all helped keep me on track. To Stacey, Lauren, Kimber, Mitch and Lady, Maggie, Lacey (also my post-its inspiration!), my family, and borrowed family members who have all just been the most encouraging – the best cheer squad I would never have known to ask for.

Writing, even in a professional context, can be at times a lonely and isolating process. I'm thankful to be able to recognise each of you as I zoom back out.

Introduction

The problem in workplace leadership is this: mindfulness and wellbeing are not seen as synonymous with being 'professional'. They are seen as a soft, even weak, way of being that exposes some kind of lack in capability in your role; no matter the role. When, in reality, leading mindfully for the wellbeing of all in our charge is a duty of care that we all have – individually, as peers and colleagues, and as leaders, managers, and business owners. Not to mention, to ourselves, if we are to create any kind of quality of life and work for us to find fulfilment and enrichment in.

But it's not a straightforward, copy-and-paste approach we can apply to every single person and every single scenario. For starters, each person's brain works differently from the next, even before we take into account neuro-differences. Each person – and their brain and body – has had different life experiences, potential recognised and unrecognised traumas, different conditioning from upbringing, has learned different things inside and outside of formal communication, and has different preferences. It makes leadership the tricky beast that it can be, and wellbeing science as challenging as it has always been. But it is also the blend of these two things that can make it all the much more rewarding. First, we must get to know ourselves and how we interact with the leadership nuances in which we exist.

In my earliest memories of recognising what leadership is, I was simultaneously learning the story that leadership did not need to mean sacrificing oneself at the altar of the position. And, like many moments of learning and growth for all of us, I learned this by watching how others in previous generations were doing it. Somehow in that moment, I had the wherewithal to recognise how much that version of leadership was definitively not for me.

I played association netball growing up. It was my chosen winter sport; we were always a sporty family, and my parents made it a point to be pretty actively involved with whatever club or association we three kids were involved in, for both our chosen summer and winter sports. We had parameters, which felt fairly appropriate; while we were encouraged to play sport and be involved, we were limited to one sport per half of the year. This was to ensure we were focusing on one thing and doing it properly, not getting distracted from school work, and for our parents, so that they weren't so busy running each

DOI: 10.4324/9781003632771-1

of us around to every sport under the sun that their own personal work and interests were diminished. These sport limitations did not extend to school-related, outside of hours activities for me, like participating in rock eisteddfod and musicals.

Being someone who apparently likes to be intensely involved and dedicated to my chosen interests, I began playing netball at the lowest age group available – the 'modifieds' J Grade team. It's the one where we six-year-olds get to start learning the foundations of the sport, how to play the game, how to catch the ball, and how to pivot (a word that will take on entirely new understandings as life goes on depending on the TV show I'm watching, or the 2020 global pandemic we are experiencing). Undiagnosed autistic and ADHD – a diagnosis that wouldn't come for another almost 30 years – I felt like I was in a safe space; my mum had volunteered to become our team coach, I had a healthy outlet for my physical and mental energy, and I got to play with a bunch of my friends. I also distinctly remembered learning what being a captain of the team meant, and unsurprisingly to me now, loved when my turn to captain came around.

Learning a sport this way also gives you the opportunity to figure out what positions you enjoy most, and even build on those skills. While we rotated around the positions enough to experience them, I mostly favoured being Goal Attack (GA). It gave me enough room to run, being an active participant in the momentum of the game, while also allowing me to be one of the two positions on the team who are allowed in the goal circle to take our shots. Once again, I liked to be everywhere.

There was something proactive about it that I enjoyed. Over the years, this same love developed and then overtook the Centre position. While I couldn't shoot when I had that bib on, playing Centre meant I was able to play a role in assisting every position on my team, whether that week's Captain or not. The label didn't matter, and that recognition has formed my fundamental belief about leadership to this day: that while we will have different or varying resources, we do not need to be titled as a 'leader' in order to show up, contribute, and lead in some way. Playing these two court positions is where I felt most useful, which only gave me even more energy to do so.

At the same time I was finding my footing in our netball club as a player working up through the grades each year, my mother was taking on positions within the netball committee: first as the association secretary and eventually the president – for multiple years running. While it can certainly be something to be proud of – for both herself, as well as for me as her daughter – the experience was actually a bit more like watching someone held hostage. At times, it felt to me like she was trapped with expectations incidentally thrust upon her to sacrifice all of her spare time and energy to the unpaid role that she, eventually and understandably, stopped wanting to be in altogether.

Yet, the expectation was that she would continue to fulfil that role year after year, thanks to the lack of any other willing contenders at that time. It is hard to make a role appealing when the impact of the stress is evident. Onlookers witness that negative wellbeing impact from inevitably trying to keep an entire association of players, coaches, umpires, and players' parents happy and satisfied, and decided that stepping into this volunteer position wasn't worth subjecting themselves to. At least in those years, as it appeared to me.

She had originally stepped into that leadership position by choice with a desire to contribute to the sporting world in which both her daughters were heavily involved, similar to our father who, too, involved himself in leading our various nippers age groups and helping out around the surf club. While Mum was coaching or leading the association, Dad was often getting up early on a Saturday morning to freshly chalk the grass netball courts for the J Grade players, long after I had moved up.

When someone feels trapped, underappreciated, and underpaid in a position that is only adding some kind of stress to their – potentially already stressful life – their only way out stops being a conversation and a negotiation, and becomes leaving the organisation entirely. A clean break where they can't be coerced back into it, and they can reset.

To this young teen brain, watching my perception of the experience play out told the lesson that leaders need to give their literal everything in order to serve, and that the only way they would let you out was to burn out, depart, and never look back. Especially if you were a female leader. Even to me at that age, this seemed an extremely illogical way to go about treating the leaders – and members – of an organisation. From a leadership and retention perspective, if your people feel like they have no choice but to flee, you're going to lose more people and spend more having to replace them than you should. In which case, you've got some improving to do somewhere within your system.

These days as a fully fledged adult, I have spent some years in volunteer elite national team management and on the board of a National Sporting Organisation, likely a result of the example set for me. Over my career thus far, I have also been in positions where I have had to lead a whole department without the title – or respect from some other managers – that gave me the authority to do so. I have been asked to manage the PR for a start-up partnership, spent dedicated time as a multi-hat wearer as the head of operations and unofficial head of wellbeing, and I have started and continue to run my own business.

Knowing what I know about leadership and, in this case, sporting committees now, I think about that club as it was back then and the impact this abrupt departure might have had on them functionally. For them to lose their stalwart President and very active association member of many years suddenly, without having the same access to her after the fact to even help transition anyone else into the role properly, or perhaps even without having anyone else willing enough *to* do so at short notice by the end of that year, I imagine would have interrupted organisational functioning at least for a time. All because of this demand put on this particular leader. And whether this demand was explicit or simply because they genuinely thought highly of this person's capabilities that it all accidentally ended up piling up, the result was the same.

This impact goes beyond just the value of any personal relationships involved as well. You can have the friendliest, most amicable relationships in any kind of workplace, and, if enough pressure is put on a leader, damage can still be incurred. Relationships are important, but all of the friendliness cannot make up for unaware demand on people in leadership positions and the impact it can have on the humans in those positions.

Whether or not this is exactly how that situation played out, what I observed at that younger age taught me a lot about how I now prioritise wellbeing in leadership positions; despite still being years away at the time from being close to understanding what that even means. From my perspective, it was an example of what being in a leadership position *could* do to you if wellbeing was not considered. Accurate to the circumstances or not, what I learned from it all came down to wellbeing. When long-standing, almost whole-family involvement could be severed because the need to get out of the stress has become so completely overwhelming, it's hard not to look to how wellbeing is so often left by the wayside in leadership positions and how it harms not only the person involved, but their teams and organisations around them as well.

This was almost 25 years ago at this point. We, thankfully, know a lot more about leadership now and hopefully, with the help of research, exploring lived experiences, and books like these, we collectively can improve that experience for both leaders and the people around them.

We cannot have professional development without personal development. There once was a time in the professional standard when that would have been vehemently argued against, and it wasn't that long ago. When we recognise leadership begins with ourselves first, it makes it easier to reflect further back than you might expect to, where those more formative lessons on leadership and wellbeing might have started to form for you.

Leadership can feel overwhelming and fraught with danger, even when it's a role you actually want to pursue. The ever-insidious imposter syndrome seems always ready to tighten its grip, often before you even reach a position of leadership. It's a kind of fraud-filled feeling that tells you that everyone else around you knows exponentially more than you do and will only *ever* know more than you do – that you can never catch up. Not only that, but also telling you that they are all looking at you, wondering why or how you got to the leadership position in the first place. It does not discriminate, nor does it wait for only when you have gone beyond your actual realm of capability. It will strike regardless of how qualified you are. It is simply present and ever-ready to tell you.

While it's usually good advice to always be looking for what you can learn from the people around you or the situations you find yourself in, imposter syndrome is there, ever-ready to hijack your best intentions. An article by Pedler (2011) suggests leadership development must include a large measure of personal development, a need further emphasised when imposter syndrome rears its head, in order to work through it and remove its limiting impacts.

Furthermore, it goes to explain that the experience of imposter syndrome itself gives us the conviction of fraudulence, developing our internal belief that one *is*, in fact, a fraud. The fear of being seen as a fraud can have you freezing up in avoidance, feeling like you can't take opportunities because you inherently believe you're never really ready for them, and even tightening your grip of control in often the most unhealthy and unhelpful ways – for you and for everyone else. Naturally, this only contributes to the stress. Herein lies our challenge.

Then, there is the fear of saying the wrong thing.

What if you get too political for someone's tastes?

What if someone disagrees with your otherwise well-thought-out direction?

What if you're still learning with people around you who may have different experiences from your own, and don't yet understand the context of why what you're saying is potentially harmful in some way to others?

This attempt at perfectionism that stops you from saying anything is only risking adding to the burden of stress, on top of the things you are already feeling stressed about. It also leads you to avoid that personal development that, as previously mentioned, is a necessary, significant part of your leadership development as you work to overcome or make peace with these things.

Not only that, it sets a poor example for those you lead. Do you want a team that is so stressed trying to make something perfect that they never really take initiative or complete tasks they need to, because they are too busy apologising and justifying in advance, 'just in case'? These teams remain stuck, instead of collaborative and progressive; even if collaboration and progression are key values and desires of theirs. If that doesn't sound useful to you, consider what your team is experiencing when you're also busy demonstrating the same perfectionistic, fraud-avoidance behaviours. Wanting your work to be of a high quality is not the same thing as keeping yourself in a box that has the stress and overwhelm volume turned up to 11.

Try as I might have, I have had to learn about this unhelpful kind of perfectionism through my own trial and error, as both a working professional in leadership and as a business owner. I had to learn that I cannot run a business that is primarily about leadership and wellbeing without speaking about some of the harder things.

Putting yourself in positions of responsibility such as leadership will often call on you to *take* responsibility and learn the lesson. The only other option will be to resist it – potentially causing yourself or others further harm. When you lean into it, you learn to do better, whether you like it or not.

Sometimes those harder things for me have consisted of what is simply walking into a room of 50 or so soldiers to talk to them about mindfulness. There were both assumptions and realities I had to confront about their willingness to even hear the content. There was every chance possible that many of the participants in this particular audience had already written off what I had to say the moment they saw 'meditation' on the schedule, and were in some cases only there because there was some kind of order passed down their chain of command to be there. Yet, if I had shown up only apologising for being there, holding back and half-heartedly sharing as if I was trying to save them from the full amount, I wouldn't have been doing my job, but I also wouldn't have been serving them adequately in my role. If I am going to be talking to them about shifting their relationship with discomfort, so they could become more comfortable with it, I was required to do the same myself. That could either happen in real time or with preparation.

One of the challenging aspects of leadership is to acknowledge that we cannot possibly *always* understand what it's like to be someone else, or have all of the experience – personal and professional – that those we lead have. In those environments, I was there to teach soldiers something that is as uncomfortable as turning their attention inward. Standing in front of a room of people trained in very different ways to me, and talking about 'acknowledging your feelings' is an experience in taking a leap into the great unknown of every possible response you may get. As a leader, you need to show up and lead despite the looks you may read on people's faces. Your audience may not always feel willing. Remember also how perception and assumption can lead you astray. We cannot know definitively what others are thinking or feeling, unless it is communicated directly.

One person, we'll call Henry, sat through eight weeks of group sessions I facilitated. He never spoke up during our sessions, never asked questions, and never sought out a conversation before or after our session times. On the very last day of that eight-week programme, he approached me on my way out to thank me, quoting something I had said to them as a group on the very first day that had apparently stuck with him. I didn't remember what I had said, or that I had said it at all. But all the while I had spent all ten sessions over eight weeks just hoping and trusting that the evidence-based work I was sharing with them was being delivered in a way that was helpful.

Approximately a year following this, I was at another event. Henry had heard I was going to be there, as was he, and sought me out to speak to me. This time he shared how much he was still applying from our sessions even a whole year later, sharing how much of a difference it had made to his mindset and his relationships not only at work, but with his family at home as well.

Each of these moments alone gave me information that helped me strengthen certain aspects of my facilitation, while also serving as a reminder that sometimes you simply won't know how it's landing. You won't always get it right, but if you ensure your information is factual and delivered as best you possibly can in each moment, you have a better chance. In the case of most 'leadership' moments, I had no way of knowing this impact otherwise. I just had to lead.

As a leader, you are called to decide what values you want to represent you. Not only are these values just as important for how you lead, they are also important for how you do business. Beyond being just a bunch of well-designed words on the wall or your video call background, values are inherently experienced through your actions.

There are certainly demonstrable ways to do business that focus only on making money and zero per cent emphasis on the human experience, much like our professional predecessors. We'll often hear of this approach even still referred to as the 'glory days' of business. These are often lamentations given, while at the same time anecdotes are shared from others on their deathbeds, wishing they didn't work so hard for people who didn't care about them, while sacrificing time with family and friends who did care.

Another more emerging, but certainly not new, way of doing business is more about people first. The 'people first' approach tends to be focused on ensuring business values are not just something pretty to put on the wall behind you, but rather something that is more actively shown through decisions, behaviours, and actions.

Either, or any other, kind of leadership then becomes a choice on values. In Brené Brown's *Dare to Lead* (Brown, 2018, p. 186), she defines values as:

> a way of being or believing that we hold most important. Living into our values means that we do more than profess our values, we practice them. We walk our talk – we are clear about what we believe and hold important, and we take care that our intentions, words, thoughts, and behaviors align with those beliefs.

We know that values can show up accidentally if you are not paying attention. These can then become representative of who you are; whether you intend them to or not. Unintentional value mismatches can occur, for example, such as someone advocating for the importance of support and awareness around mental health, only to then bully their colleagues, those they manage, or even unsuspecting people on the internet with their snarky words and attempts at 'hot takes' and 'gotcha moments'.

Values mismatches like these do not always have to be malicious in intent. You might find that any of your values-to-actions mismatches are based simply on not taking the time to notice. It is similar, if you will, to values that are passed down from parents or mentors. When we are young, particularly, we are more likely to take on the values of those around us because that is what we learn in our formative years. Acclimatising to our communities and attempting to fit in is also how we as a species inherently learn how to keep ourselves safe.

The unsuspecting demonstration of values happens in business when we fail to consider the impacts of our behaviour, those things we stand for, or even processes we put in place. As a leader, you may desire to have an inclusive workplace, for example. Beyond what may already be legislated, you may have a desire to be more proactive in ensuring it is a very clearly welcoming workplace. However, when you have barriers in procedures or processes that limit your people or exclude them, whether you mean to or not, the value you are actually demonstrating and upholding might be one more akin to exclusion or non-supportive. The opposite of what you have said you desire. It doesn't mean that you're necessarily a 'bad' person, or that there is a judgement required. It does mean it's important for you to take a deeper look at how you follow through, despite your best intentions.

Leadership requires courage and the willingness to lean into discomfort. Leading, and therefore your values, is about noticing and reflecting, which can contribute to discomfort. It is about calling yourself to account for your words and behaviours, for yourself and for your leadership. It is about holding yourself responsible for any adjustments, outcomes, and actions required. While many see this as 'punishment', this is simply a natural consequence of how you've shown up; something you can repair. You will not always get it right all of the time or every time, and that is the part that can make people feel fearful. When you take responsibility for how you're showing up, regardless of how imperfectly, and regardless of how much you are still learning, that will speak volumes in relation to how your values are carried out. When you do this part intentionally, you get to choose the track that is playing at that volume.

Leadership requires you to get comfortable with being uncomfortable. It won't necessarily make the discomfort go away, especially not immediately, but it can lessen the resistance you have to it. This way you can get busy leading yourself down the path – or creating an entirely new one.

There is a mindfulness at play in this buildable skill we know of as emotional intelligence, and that mindfulness requires a willingness for inner reflection, and a follow-through on doing something useful with that awareness you develop. Notice there is often a difference between being 'ready' to do this kind of work and being 'willing' to. Too often we are met with examples where we believe we must get ourselves 'ready' first before we take the leap of action to do something, anything. Anecdotally, most parents will tell you that even if their desire was strong to have children, they never necessarily felt completely, one hundred per cent 'ready' – at some point they just had to take the chance and hope they would figure it out along the way.

This pressure often comes from within our own selves, where the action we think we need to be taking could be very different from what we already 'know' at this point; those things we 'know' based on what's been modelled for us in leadership and mindfulness previously. Or what we 'know' could even be things, or something, that has not been modelled for you previously at all, but you've developed an understanding of based on that lack of modelling. An example of this lack might be never having the example set of a leader who proactively checks in with individual members of the team. Even without the conscious awareness of the lack of action, what you might have developed in so far as what you 'know' about leadership could be that 'leaders stay separate from their team'.

You are invited to consider your willingness as an equally, if not more so, valuable currency than 'readiness' to how you choose to learn about and do – perform – *your* leadership. Your willingness is what creates the way forward for the readiness, not the other way around. Your willingness to show up for the tough conversations with yourself. Your willingness to then turn that into potentially vulnerable conversations with others; which can also feel tough.

It is all a necessary and essential part of leadership and being a truly effective leader. Leadership goes beyond just the prestige of the title and accolades, and asks you to take the necessary action and behavioural steps each day. Every day.

Leadership asks you to step into *being* a leader.

And that is where our work lies.

Setting the Stage: What to Expect in This Book

Leadership in the modern workplace demands more than just technical expertise. In order to navigate team disconnectedness, the complexity of dynamics, and teams that require different things to inspire and motivate them than even the last decade, modern workplace leaders require emotional intelligence and mindful presence for this role. But just like these technical skills you have already developed didn't happen overnight or without some attention and effort, neither will the skills that have long been called 'soft', but are anything but that.

Shifts in workplace culture, office versus hybrid dynamics, legislative requirements around employee wellbeing, personal economic, emotional and mental pressures, and both leaders and employees desiring to feel more purpose have all amplified the demand for tools that develop more resilience and empathy. People are, rightly, no longer satisfied to simply show up to work and burn themselves out. People want to thrive in whatever their role is and feel more satisfied in their time at work. Leaders are navigating the challenges that can come from burnout and disengagement in themselves and their team members and need the support to understand how to step into this new era of leadership.

This book is intended to be a bridge, taking concepts within academic research and applying them to the lived experience of those who are practitioners in their fields. It will therefore explore the relationship between those two worlds, using information as we understand it from research in the areas of wellbeing, mindfulness, emotional intelligence, leadership, empathy, and beyond. It will also provide contextual examples of how you can spot the signs of areas that need more support and how to actually begin going about it.

To live in the world of being a practitioner of your work is a different requirement from being an academic iin your field. While many people are multi-modal and straddle each of these skills over the course of their careers, this book is written from the perspective of the practicality it requires of balancing your job role while also expanding your learning around it. So whether you are only just entering your career and want to begin building your foundations as a leader, or are looking to step out of your current burnout cycle and understand a more supportive version of leadership, even if it's different from how you've been trained so far in your career, this book provides a foundational framework of practice to assist you in getting started.

1 The Foundations of Modern Leadership

Just like building a house or a skyscraper, the foundation of the build is the most important thing to get structured and set in first. Nothing else happens before that foundation is set in (sometimes literal) stone.

For those of us uninitiated in the construction process, we might notice construction companies spending most of their time on the bigger projects on the foundation before anything else goes into place. If you have ever spent time at the window of an office, gazing out just watching it all happen, you can see how long it looks like *nothing* is happening when construction is at the foundation stage.

'Why are they taking so long doing nothing?'

'Why can't I see any progress?'

What looks a lot like 'nothing' to us construction laypeople is what can – sometimes literally – make or break the integrity of what is then built upon it, especially should it come up against any adversarial conditions that threaten it.

When you are undertaking the kind of personal development, whether it is for personal reasons or the kind that contributes to your professional development and growth, it can feel a lot like this stage. This is often why many people attempt to skip over it when they don't see the immediate results. This can also be the reason many people in business and organisations choose not to invest in it: we are so conditioned in business to go for what gives us the immediate, visible results and return on investment, that this foundational work has been unfairly devalued and divested from, at great expense. That perception has also spread to personal development more for the sake of personal, than explicit professional, development. This hustle, quick-results culture has bled into our personal lives so that it has become harder to prioritise key foundational work if the results are not greatly visible and immediate. This inner work often yields results that are more about our experience in any given environment, which then can contribute to how we perform in that environment, which is often devalued in the investment discussions because there isn't a straight line on the board.

Consider your leadership skills foundational for the growth to come; growth that holds steady all of the possibilities of your life and work experience. You

DOI: 10.4324/9781003632771-2

have two options: you can leave your foundation as the dirt that is already there; a plot of land that is as yet untended to, or perhaps existing only based on what has happened to it over its own course of history – a history that may not have anything to do with what you even need it for. Or you can purposefully cultivate it. You can ensure that it is crafted, moulded, impacted, and strengthened so that it is solid in just the way that you need it to be. In a way it is able to hold and provide the basis of the support you need in which to grow, thrive, influence as a leader, and even expand.

The only difference is that sometimes you are already well into having built your building, and when it comes to skills like leadership and developing the mindfulness and emotional intelligence that strengthens a foundation, instead of building this foundation from scratch, you are able to go back and build these skills upon your own existing foundations. These changes won't necessarily topple your entire building the way it might in real life construction, but it may make it look a bit different from what you are used to. Change can feel threatening, but this difference could possibly be even more of a fit for you and your needs now than it was before. Think of it as a renovation that makes you see a space with brand new eyes and a fresh perspective; that 'oh wow, I never knew this was possible' moment when you change a paint colour, remove a wall, or even just re-arrange the furniture.

Just like making these changes to a physical structure, it may not always feel comfortable. It can be the kind of discomfort that makes you wonder whether the effort is worth it (spoiler: like most things in work and in life, if you keep the long term in mind, it will be worth it).

It can be hard at times to see the proverbial forest for the trees, where you're in the mess of the renovation or build, before you can see the finished picture. It's like doing a spring clean of your garage – you've got to get a lot of the clutter out into the open and lay actual eyes on it, before you can process through it all, choosing what you'll do with each piece, and eventually tidy it all up again.

This is why leadership itself is ever-evolving. We learn, we unlearn, we iterate, we adjust, and we – often – learn again. Just like any good software programme; except we aren't software. We are real life, honest to goodness humans with complex brains. Remembering to start with building, or firming up, your foundation will support you as you learn new concepts and ideas, and graciously unlearn those methods that are now more outdated for what you need moving forward.

The Changing Landscape of Leadership

Leadership has always been in a state of evolution. How we lead now is different to how we led in the 1980s. How we led then was different to how we led in the 1800s. How we led *then* was different to how the Roman Empire led; and so on, going back for as long as humans have existed. It is at the very core of human nature – and nature itself – to continually evolve, and this goes just as much for ideas and concepts in both theory and practice that determine our experiences.

At the same time, each leadership style throughout history has its notable strengths and limitations, most likely brought about as a response to the circumstances of their time. This speaks to the ongoing need for evolution. As we learn more, we can then adapt more. Except in the case of business, we have begun adapting our systems and externals, attempting to 'hack' our way into optimisation, at the risk of foregoing much-needed internal adaptation to a changing world, changing needs, and new information.

In some ways, this kind of adaptation is innate in humans. In the same way that we become used to having certain people around, or immersed in certain cuisines, we tend to adapt to those aspects of our daily, or regular, lives. Our taste buds adjust to certain milk – or milk substitute – flavours, and our responses to the people around us adjust as we learn more about who they are and their own unique tones and languages they may use.

For example, someone uses the 'thumbs up' emoji in conversation and it makes you feel all sorts of things. You might feel like they're being distant with you, or dismissive of you, or even passive-aggressive. Then you get to know that person and their interaction style better, and understand a bit more how they see and use it – we discover that some people will use the 'thumbs up' as an efficient and even literal depiction of agreement. What to one person is considered rude is seen as efficient and benign to another. In a toneless, online world, there is so much meaning that can be made beyond the moment.

It is your perception that adapts once you learn what *their* perception is. Once that happens, you get to re-negotiate your response by recognising that your reaction does not match the actual circumstance, just the circumstance you thought it was. It also becomes easier, because you're not making up stories just to fill in the meaning. You have the ease of connecting it back to the human being who made the gesture. This creates more ease in the connection because instead of internalising a story, you're recognising the relationship first.

Early leadership theories within the 20th century, from approximately the 1900 to the 1940s (Fundação Getulio Vargas (Brazil), Université de Bordeaux (France) et al., 2022) focus on a period that holds a fundamental belief that effective leaders were born with certain inherent qualities. That you were 'born a leader'. It suggests that the qualities we recognised then, and recognise now, in effective leadership are not buildable skills at all, but something that you were either lucky enough to be born with, or unlucky enough to never possess, thus failing to be good enough for a leadership position. This concept suggests that it speaks to a certain kind of charisma and control being *the* leadership quality.

This is on display if we were to look historically at the world leaders that rose to and held power in the first half of the 20th century. Those in power tended to be more authoritarian leaders, such as Joseph Stalin, who led a totalitarian state in the Soviet Union for almost 30 years until his death in 1954. Other notable authoritarians were Benito Mussolini, who held Italy under a fascist regime for 21 years, when he was overthrown in 1943 as a result of the political unrest during World War II. Adolf Hitler, who led the rise of the Nazi Party in pre-war Germany, was elected Chancellor in 1933. His rise in popularity is attributed, arguably, to charisma and his 'natural born' leadership skills, which saw him take advantage of a disenfranchised post-World War I Germany. His dictatorial rule over Germany and areas of Eastern Europe spread authoritarian ideologies that ultimately led to World War II. His involvement only ended with his suicide less than two weeks before Germany surrendered, ultimately ending the war.

Interestingly enough, not all of these authoritarian leaders 'play' well with each other. While at times their rhetoric and charisma have been used to team up against their common enemy – most apparently, democracy – it was also used against each other. Joseph Stalin, while dangerously authoritarian himself, and the Soviets played a major role in fighting back against the Nazi advancement in Europe. Authoritarianism has no friends.

Authoritarianism is by no means exclusive to that first half of the 20th century alone. While we still, and have since, witnessed more examples of authoritarian leadership styles, it became more widely evident in the aftermath of World War II that much of the world is more sceptical of leadership styles that invoke charisma and the belief iin leadership skills that are 'born with' or 'born without', which perhaps marks the beginning of a shift in our understanding of leadership capacity in modern times. The natural limitation of this approach to leadership – being that you are either born possessing inherent leadership characteristics or you are not – is its lack of recognition in how systemic factors will influence the development of these characteristics. This was a turning point in understanding how leadership skills are less so traits, and more in fact buildable skills. So we evolved.

Personal leadership styles then began to be more explored, particularly over the 1950–1960s time period. This emerging style introduced us to the types of leadership models we still reference today: autocratic, democratic, and laissez-faire. This was a positive development for the fact that it allowed for a more nuanced understanding of leadership to begin to emerge. This development started to recognise that different situations will call for a different leadership approach by you in order to effectively achieve the outcome you are actually looking for.

It had a long way to go still at this point – and arguably still does even today – but in reflection, it can be noticed in the leadership differences of Dwight D. Eisenhower, John F. Kennedy, and Lyndon B. Johnson who, over the course of the two decades of United States presidential leadership in the 1950s and 1960s, each had a particular style based on the situations they were facing politically that demonstrated the blend of charismatic leadership with personal leadership style. Johnson's successor, Richard Nixon, who began his presidency in 1969, then went on to further demonstrate that personal leadership styles are only as effective as the core values of the leader displaying them. Sometimes good leadership is revealed when contrasted against poor examples.

This concept of personal leadership styles is something that was extended into the 1970s–1980s, where situational leadership thrived. By this stage, in stark contrast to the first half of the century, it was more broadly accepted that effective leadership was contingent upon situational context and specific circumstances. This introduced a recognised need for more adaptability and flexibility within leadership, which suggests an awareness – whether conscious or not – that leadership abilities can be grown, and that an awareness of situations would be required. This situational awareness could be linked to the need for some emotional intelligence, although that wording and concept was not in use at this point in history. While now it is easy for us to look back from our vantage point in knowledge and wonder where exactly that leadership adaptability was in our more public representatives as our most visual leaders, unlike earlier decades of the same century, this period highlighted the importance of flexibility in leadership. Much of this we can only know mostly from the gift of hindsight, and it is not to say that this was a focal point in the experience of leadership. It is only when we can take more of a macro view in our reflection of history that we can begin to recognise where shifts started to occur, even if smaller, more minute in scale.

The 1990–2000s time period brought around the motivational and transformational leadership styles. This is where we begin to see the most similarities and likenesses to the practices of effective leadership we know today. The focus here begins to shift from leaders simply managing tasks to more emphasis on developing relationships with those they lead; the intention being to lead to higher levels of engagement and performance. Like all things, this has been a slow burn with slow uptake as it has filtered down through the hierarchies of business. Once anecdotally thought to be only for Wall Street and Corporate America, sales type, Australian businesses for the most part seemed to spend a lot of this time distancing themselves from this style of leadership. This might be for fear of appearing to be more self-important than they think they should be, since motivational and transformational leadership naturally requires an element of being willing to achieve, or being seen really trying to achieve. Tall Poppy Syndrome is a phenomenon, quite prominent in Australia, that looks down on individuals, leaders, business owners, or executives alike who are seen to be 'trying too hard'. Yet, motivational leadership and transformational styles ask leaders to actually try and be seen as trying. That is part of the inspiration that makes the style as effective as it has been. With any particular style, it will have its flaws; some leadership moments do not require a version of motivation or transformation, but something else, and some people are not *motivated* by this particular style by their leaders. Some also feel it encourages too much competitiveness for their preference. What originally developed as a leadership style designed to foster environments of trust and collaboration by way of encouraging personal and professional growth amongst team members, instead was, perhaps, misunderstood and in some cases mis-implemented as an opportunity for competitiveness. It is as if *trying* to be successful was likened to trying to be 'cool' in the schoolyard. It risks creating a hierarchical structure of being the best, when there can only be one 'best' when it all comes down to it at the end of the day.

Now, with positive psychology and wellbeing science and research beginning to really hit its stride since emerging in the late 90s, we are learning more about how systems impact our performance, and the importance of emotional intelligence, mindfulness, and language in leadership settings.

So while evolving your own leadership can potentially be an overwhelming idea – or in some perspectives, an unnecessary burden – if you look to the more broad strokes of history, it is a lot simpler to see how necessary a function evolving leadership styles really is. While we can acknowledge that no iteration is perfect, the way we evolve, grow, and learn is by taking what we recognise as working well and trying it from there. Even while frameworks are demonstrated, even throughout this book, it is still going to remain a personal, subjective experience. Professional development does not happen *without* personal development.

One thing that is important to remember is: when looking to history, make sure you are not comparing yourself *with* history. We know the saying 'Rome wasn't built in a day', and that goes just as aptly for how we develop our own self-leadership. This understanding of mindfulness and the cultivation of emotional intelligence does not just happen because of a decision. Like all things, particularly in leadership, expect it to take time, practice, consistency, a lot of mistakes, effort, and grace.

Where leadership once was an individualistic pursuit of 'success', it has now developed more widely into a recognised role in service of the group as a whole. Here we explore that balance; how your individual actions, behaviours, and internal enquiries are for you, *and* simultaneously for everyone around you.

The Case for Emotional Intelligence and Mindfulness

A 24-year-old woman named Aleesha once found herself stuck on an hour-long phone call with a director of a different department to hers within the same organisation. This director had no particular say over her role. Aleesha reported directly to the Managing Director, one of the owners, and the intention of this set-up was that she and this other director would work together, with Aleesha's role supporting his department just as much as it supported every other department. Unfortunately, by the behaviour of this other director, Aleesha's experience was that he believed her role to be at his department's every whim, and that he was entitled to be more in charge of Aleesha and her role overall.

This hour-long call began with him calling Aleesha up in frustration about why she had not done something for his department soon enough for his liking. Aleesha's challenge was that she had already communicated to his department that she needed specific information from them to do her side of the task. This seemed obvious because their roles were situated at the forefront of that area of the business and with the clients, so naturally they would have more insight into useful information than she would, being in an internal role that was not client-facing. Instead of looking at the context, this director was instead caught up in his own story and subsequent stress of what appeared to Aleesha to be about a lack of control; something that was then projected on to her for a whole hour at a time. This director was so focused on being right that he was talking in circles instead of actually being effective with his time as one of the leaders and one of the higher-paid employees in the business. At no point did he suggest to Aleesha that he was looking for a solution other than the one he had already pre-decided upon. Unfortunately for him, she was not in the position of authority to change the whole company structure, nor was it a useful spend of time for either of them.

Aleesha is somebody who self-confesses to not naturally enjoying conflict or heated debate. She finds it challenging to find the balance between expressing a point of view, facts and data, or perspective clearly and strongly enough, and then feeling bad that she might have completely shut down someone else's opinion with those facts and data; something that she became only more aware could be impacted and made even more challenging as an autistic person when she was later diagnosed. When this particular conversation happened, it was earlier in her professional career, so it was also one of the first real, significant times in her working experience she had been presented with such a confrontation. Given this natural challenge, despite all of her previous study and training, as well as her overall greenness to the experience at the time, this moment stands out. Almost by accident, in response to his steady hum of bullying language and belligerence over the length of the phone call, she found herself settling into this almost flow state of clarity and perspective.

In a study on flow state in high-performance athletes, Harris et al. (2017) describe flow state, often referred to as being 'in the zone', as a mental condition where an individual experiences complete absorption and focused engagement in an activity, particularly during high-pressure situations like competition. Neither Aleesha nor this director in this phone call were elite athletes, but it did possess a competitive, high-stakes feel in the experience. According to Harris et al., flow state involves an effortlessness amidst demand, where the increased challenge is inexplicably met with a feeling of effortlessness, in paradox to the high pressure. Flow state can result in the individual feeling as if their performance is heightened, potentially as a result of this effortlessness. Actions can feel clearer and more automatic, allowing for quicker decision-making without conscious, time-expending deliberation. This goes along with the intense focus and concentration described in flow state, involving a laser-like focus on the activity, competition, or moment. In the study, it was described as concentrated attention and presence enhancing the athlete's ability to react to dynamic situations, allowing them to maintain performance amidst the chaos of the competition.

This state might be possible to experience wherever you might feel that pressure of heightened performance. What is particularly helpful in responding to this pressure that Aleesha said she experienced was a loss of self-consciousness. She reported being so present and immersed in the phone conversation, the attempted journey to the solution, and staying laser-focused on the point instead of getting side-swept by any perceived or actual insults, that she did not have the anxiety in the moment of wondering about the perception of others in how she was handling it. While this director was comfortably in a small, private office in another state, she was in an open-plan office surrounded by up to about 20 of her colleagues across a variety of other departments who could hear her side of the conversation only, and yet her concern was somehow focused not on them. It was on the solution.

They also described time distortion in the experience of flow state – where individuals report feeling that their ability to quickly process information and respond was improved, as if they had more time than what was actually occurring. That hour-long phone conversation did not feel like an hour at the time, even though many people have experienced many different long phone conversations in other contexts that they've certainly felt every minute of. It was only after the fact that Aleesha became aware of the length of time, and the mental exhaustion as a result.

Instead of getting caught up in his emotions and ways of expressing, which is so easy to do when we communicate with other human beings, she found herself detaching from his reactions and tone. She acknowledged his frustrations, then gave him her perception of what the ideal outcomes were. Aleesha was then able to ask him what he thought the ideal outcome would or should be, regardless of *how* it came about. This gave her the opportunity to offer his side of responsibility in the matter over to him without the need for the 'gotcha' moment many confrontations tempt us with.

It turned out his idea of the ideal outcome actually matched hers. What made it into such a long conversation, however, was his insistence on circling back to his frustrations instead of landing in that happy place of agreement and letting them stay there, to then move forward. His stresses, while we can empathise, were his own in that moment and they were getting in the way of progress.

So continued the repetition of the conversation: he would vent *at* Aleesha, she would acknowledge and then express her understanding of the outcomes, before asking him his. He would essentially agree, resulting in her internal relief, naively thinking that maybe they were getting somewhere this time. Aleesha's suggested way forward was quickly rebutted when she offered it, with another onslaught of his same frustrations.

Circling over and over.

Aleesha wasn't necessarily aware of the process she was working in during this conversation. It's only in retrospect and after more training in areas of communication, mindfulness, and leadership in her career that she's been able to recognise how it was playing out. It happened by what felt like accident.

Due to her inexperience, Aleesha did not yet have the skills in understanding when to shut this kind of conflict down so they could actually move forward. She was, and sometimes still admits to being prone to getting caught up in the desire for resolving things right there and then. What she did not know enough then to be mindful of was when someone's apparent stress is high enough, even when you can get them to partly acknowledge agreement in some way, there is not always a path forward in that moment. Without laying too much unhelpful judgement on herself, if she had possessed more effective leadership skills and the required authority in that moment, she might have known to kindly – for both of them – cut it short after the second, or at latest third, go around, well before the hour mark. The awareness to recognise when you have gone as far as you can in this moment with another person is sometimes beneficial to the situation you are trying to overcome and the outcome you are trying to achieve. The reality of the scenario was a challenge due to the power imbalance between Aleesha, who at that time was only a couple of years graduated from university and into her professional career, and him, who was a middle-aged man with the title and years to outweigh her own authority. It also did not seem to give him much of a willingness to see a different perspective other than the one that had apparently meant so much to him.

This power imbalance needs to be considered in all cases of leadership, in all scenarios as they arise. While there is no age limit or title required for any of us to step into leadership, it is often the case that people, particularly in the corporate workplace, are not given the authority and subsequent respect that, in some cases, unfortunately, only comes with that authority, to lead in a significant way. For Aleesha in this scenario, while she reported to the Managing Director, as this director did in his own line of authority, she was only able to hold her ground so far. Their titles were mismatched for the conversation and his approach, his of 'Director' and hers, understandably given her experience, as 'Coordinator'. While leadership is not always led from the top down *only* – I am a big proponent of cross-level leadership and collaboration – this did make this particular event a bit harder for her to navigate a way out of. The benefit of it being she can share about it now in her own leadership role to help others, having learned from that very experience.

In addition to all of this, there is no way of knowing what else this director had going on outside of this scenario that could have been influencing how he was reacting *at* her. Had they collectively known more about emotional intelligence long before that moment – and had it already been more normalised in workplace culture rather than still existing as a seemingly contentious and optional point of view – both Aleesha *and* him, as well as many others like them who have experienced similar or worse frustrations in the workplace, could have been spared the stress. We can only improve and do things better once we know better. Most often that opportunity is left for what comes in the future rather than being able to impact what has already happened in the past.

While Aleesha can feel proud of how she handled herself in this extremely challenging conversation, without having had any prior time to prepare notes, talking points, or even to pre-emptively calm herself, she still ended the call feeling drained and as if she had fought some kind of battle. Ultimately, she did receive the validation and recognition of a whole office full of colleagues who had also had to sit there listening to her side of the conversation for the whole hour. She was gifted a lot of verbal or even literal pats on the back once she hung up the phone, but that only supported her ego, not the circumstance. It was still not enough to undo the stress and unnecessary energy expenditure that she feels sure resulted in a distinct lack of productivity for the rest of the day; not least to mention how she also felt and its impact on her quality of life while at work.

If both of them were able to be more mindful of how what they were feeling was impeding the progress of the conversation, they might have been able to adjust our respective approaches and reach our shared goals sooner with much more ease, and much less lost productivity. There are some studies that indicate that mindfulness training and practices can improve productivity by as much as 20-30 per cent, with employees who practise mindfulness often found to be more focused and efficient in their tasks (Baer, 2011). This kind of efficiency could have been more front of mind had mindfulness been more known of, mainstream and integrated within workplace culture from earlier on. The business itself would have benefitted by avoiding this whole scenario entirely and more focused on finding a solution to move forward with. Sometimes two, seemingly, opposing parties can still want the same outcome, but not know how to make their way to the outcome without some help.

So What Is Mindfulness Then?

How do we define mindfulness, so that we can then recognise it and harness it for our overall greater good within our lives and our workplaces? Far from being a so-called 'woo woo' concept that is deemed only for people who live in the forest or on a mountain, it is a research-backed practice and a knowledge that can support us as a society, both individually and collectively however we gather – at work, at home, with our respective villages. What is the point otherwise in professional – and personal – development, if not to improve our quality of life?

Choi et al. (2021) defines mindfulness as being aware and engaged with your present experiences, actively dealing with your thoughts and feelings, and using this awareness to navigate life's challenges rather than seeking quick fixes for stress. This definition of mindfulness helps to put words to a concept that is often misunderstood, misrepresented, and misinformed. It instead presents a tangible practice of continually bringing your attention back to the present moment and what is showing up *now*, and offers a way to use it to build up your ability to experience more ease in life, even in difficult or challenging moments. In defining this concept and practice of mindfulness, it asks us not necessarily to 'slow down' or empty our minds, but to redirect them long enough to what we can notice now.

What is happening right now, in this moment?

What is right in front of me?

What can I perceive with my available senses? Smell, sight, touch, taste, sound – whichever of these is available for you to access in each moment.

On the surface, it seems like the antithesis to modern working and success culture. How do we slow down enough to do this, when we want the success momentum to speed up? There are a lot of people who assume that losing the tried and tested ways of 'leaving your feelings at the door', the hustle culture of pushing through, and ignoring our own stress and the impacts it has on us perhaps as martyrdom in the workplace, will ruin productivity and success when we use mindfulness in the name of no longer attempting to sweep it all under the rug. It's no wonder there can be so much resistance to the entire idea of mindfulness within these professional contexts; it all looks on the outside like a lot of work without the guarantee or the immediacy of payoff. It also looks like a lot of work that distracts from the real business of making money.

What if the alternative was true, instead? What if both encouraging and integrating a practice of personal and workplace mindfulness could create a version of efficiency that, while perhaps feeling somewhat unfamiliar to 'business as usual', actually created a harmony within the structures of an organisation? There was a study by Alkoby et al. (2018) that found that employees who participated in mindfulness training reported a 30 per cent reduction in stress and anxiety levels. This is a significant percentage that, if able to be replicated, would result in a significant difference for a workplace or organisation that might already be feeling the squeeze of stress. Particularly in times of economic and political challenge.

For ease of round numbers, let's imagine you have ten staff members who are all some flavour of stressed. As per this study, this result doesn't mean that exactly three out of those ten people were suddenly not stressed when they participated in mindfulness training. Instead, it suggests that each of those ten people would, statistically, feel about 30 per cent less intensity in their stress. The volume of all 10 of those people was turned down approximately 30 per cent each.

It is important to remember that the results also do not indicate exact figures, per exact person. There is no guarantee that every single person involved in the practice would experience an exact 30 per cent reduction. There *may* be some who experience more and some who experience less in their results, resulting in an averaging out of 30 per cent. Even still, with this amount of stress reduction across the workforce overall, it would still make a significant, arguably positive, impact in the wider organisational view.

Other studies indicated that companies that implement mindfulness programmes may notice a decrease in staff turnover rates. While speculative, there could be a connection between, for example, the decrease in stress and staff having the capacity and willingness to continue in their roles at their current place of employment. Not having the cost of replacing staff members, including the cost of advertising, the productivity lost in the handover and re-training, the time spent interviewing and onboarding, not to mention the cost of potentially having that role empty until the right fit was found, would be significant for a business that was functioning well otherwise.

When mindfulness programmes have research to show us they can lead to such a significant reduction in stress levels, what other reason would organisations have to continue dismissing the research-based evidence that it could be a significantly impactful supportive measure for their team? Imagine being able to improve the quality of the time people have at work, and help to not only support the organisation's bottom line, but to improve it, by prioritising a practice, and sometimes education, of mindfulness within the company culture that benefits all.

The Role Emotional Intelligence Plays

Long assumed to be an innate trait that somebody either has, or does not have, emotional intelligence is a far more buildable skill than it has been given credit for outside of the academic realm of those who spend their days – and nights – learning to understand it better. Yet, it has not made it all that more embraced within organisations without considerable effort. The struggle with mainstreaming mindfulness into leadership and workplaces could be linked to a presence, or lack of, emotional intelligence; it is after all going to require the emotional intelligence to recognise where there is a need for more support measures like mindfulness to address things like stress.

While there is not necessarily a universally accepted, precise definition of what emotional intelligence is amongst researchers, Krén and Séllei (2020) suggest that emotional intelligence can be seen as an umbrella term referencing personal competence regarding handling one's own emotions and the emotions of others, which ultimately influences decision-making and interpersonal interactions.

I like to explain it as: emotional intelligence is a buildable skill that helps you to recognise, understand, and respond more usefully to your own emotions as well as to the emotions of others. When in a workplace environment, it can inform more progressive and supportive decision-making and improve interpersonal interactions and relationships, even when under stress.

This can also be the result outside of workplace environments. When we practise and develop emotional intelligence in one area, it naturally positively influences us in other areas. When you work on having a self-awareness of stress and how you respond to it at work, you are more likely to naturally transfer that skill to your home life. When you develop your listening-to-understand skills at home, your ability to comprehend information at work should improve too; which could naturally extend to your ability to follow through and deliver on certain tasks more effectively, with more clarity.

I discovered this unintentionally during a particular season in my life, that also happened to coincide with the first year of the COVID-19 pandemic. Many relationships across the world were naturally challenged during this time, both in the personal and professional realms. Personal relationships were challenged because many were either thrust together into their homes 24/7, in a way they might not have been accustomed to prior, or unable to connect in person in the way they might have normally. Professional relationships were challenged when many forms of communication suddenly became virtual. Text format, whether in email or messaging services, rarely adequately conveys tone. Calendars were filled up with back-to-back video meetings, where the human brain is using more energy to make up for the lack of evident body language that we subconsciously take in when we are communicating with others. When we can only see someone's shoulders and upwards – if even that – it puts an additional strain on the brain to try to match what minimal body language it is able to perceive, with tone, facial expression, and *then* the actual words that were being said. Not to mention the entire global pandemic happening outside of our doors, and in most cases inside of our homes at times as well, and the health implications of that naturally adding to the feelings of stress.

At this time, I remember struggling with communicating clearly with some of my close friends who lived overseas, and that I was not able to see in person with it being unsafe to travel and Australia's borders being closed. The combination of stress of a global pandemic, in my case suddenly being overwhelmed with a lot of work projects in my field of business – otherwise a blessing, but slightly overwhelming at the same time – political uncertainty with the upcoming US Presidential Election, and the languishing in uncertainty that many, if not all, of us were subject to thanks to this global fever were all piling onto me. I started struggling with how to convey how I felt or what I wanted. It felt like it didn't matter whether I said what I was feeling anyway because I had no power to change any of the bigger contributing causes, and it seemed useless to say what I wanted because, again, I could not take certain key action steps at the time that would get me there. Worst of all, for me at the time at least, I was noticing the same in some of these friends.

There was a disconnect. At the same time, there was also a frustration because of the desire to still connect, but not quite knowing how to communicate through all of these external stressors outside of our direct control. So I tried to practise what I preached and support clients with – by taking my own medicine and leading by example. The intention was not to necessarily change, control or manipulate anyone else's behaviour. It was simply the only thing I knew how to do – communicate in ways I wish I was being communicated with.

It can be awkward changing up some of your language with your nearest and dearest, even if the effect is you improving getting the words out more clearly.

Going in with the intention of removing my unintended attempt to control how others were communicating with me, and instead to be more deliberate in practising communication styles I aspired to helped me to recognise a few key things.

One was that I developed a bit more patience again, at a time globally where tolerances were feeling stretched, which helped me to connect more instead of reacting. Another was the recognition that their reactions did not necessarily have anything to do with me, but that I could invite – not force – an open dialogue by being more open myself. Another, and almost what feels like the most important realisation, was the acceptance that not only are we all going to make mistakes along the way, even when we are genuinely trying, but it is also OK that we do make mistakes – so long as we practise recognising them, and repairing them.

Then the most interesting thing happened. By changing my language in how I would describe things, or check in on others and ask questions that were more thoughtfully worded, I began to notice that they had started to do the same. Again, to be clear for if and when you might try replicating this approach – there was no expectation on my end that *they* would change. It was just an attempt to do better with my own adjustments. For example, it was the simplicity of beginning to use more statements like 'I am feeling' or 'I am noticing' ahead of describing reactions, instead of just being in the reaction.

Instead of seeming irrationally irritable and responding with 'I'm fine, it's just…' and never really able to finish the sentence in a useful way, I began to attempt explaining the actual experience. 'I feel spikey and I am unsure why' helped other people understand and hear it more directly, even if there was no answer or solution available, instead of having them deal with the mood and tone in words that might leave them with the onus of having to guess if, and what, might be wrong.

I believe that perhaps the reason that emotional intelligence is sometimes difficult to pin down with a definition is that, at least in some part, it depends on the environment and the words you might use for each context. Emotional intelligence in a personal, more intimate relationship might use different words to describe it than how emotional intelligence in a professional workplace may be described:

> Emotional intelligence is a buildable skill that helps you to recognise, understand, and respond more usefully to your own emotions as well as the emotions of others.

The wording of 'buildable skill' is more at home in a workplace environment, where skills-building is commonplace jargon and practice; it is almost expected in both a regular and long-term career capacity. These words, however, may not be as commonly used in your more intimate relationships. Perhaps the word 'ability' would help it feel more at ease in a personal environment. Ultimately it means the same thing, but semantics tend to mean something to the audience and inform how they are then able to grasp not just the concept of it, but the practice too.

The mistake here is the assumption that just because it is different words, it means that the benefits operate within neatly confined silos of our lives. It creates more silos. There is a mistake often made by many corporate workers who believe that their emotional intelligence is linked to how well they network. *Networking* is its own skill in itself and certainly requires a depth of social skills for it to be effective and the connection to possess genuineness. All of this is very beneficial when it comes to relating to others and building your business or career over time, particularly with more external stakeholders. The risk is believing that those networking people skills naturally equate to emotional intelligence. In a Venn diagram between the two, networking and emotional intelligence would certainly have a crossover somewhere, to some degree, in the middle. But your people skills must go beyond your ability to work a room. Your people skills, particularly internally within your workplace, must require the internal work of self-awareness first. We cannot recognise in others what we have not built the capacity to acknowledge in ourselves.

This applies equally to different causations that might create the same, or similar, emotional experience. Somebody who understands the grief of losing a parent, for example, may be able to recognise and acknowledge somebody else's grief of saying goodbye to a beloved pet. They do not need to have had the same experience, or even equate it the same way, in order to recognise the emotional experience occurring. They do not need to understand what it is like to lose a pet, or what that attachment feels like with a pet, to acknowledge that somebody is grieving in the same capacity that others feel grief. So when this shows up in a workplace – and it will, because we are all living very human lives – this practice of emotional intelligence helps us to navigate it far better and more effectively than the awkward condolences and misunderstandings that can arise out of the uncertainty.

A Unified Framework for Thriving Leadership

We need a more unified framework on which we build leadership that determines success in an updated way; a framework that allows the individual to thrive with less likelihood of burning out, at least in regard to the factors that they can control, as well as a framework that leadership thriving *also* includes teams thriving as a result. Less of the silos that have previously, and still in some ways insidiously, prioritise the individual over the group, and more of an approach that recognises the experiences of the individuals *within* the group, including leaders and including each team member, and understands how that can play out in the ecosystem of workplaces, teams, and organisations in any manner. So that when leaders thrive, we are more able to trust that that experience is passed through from leader to team, with no 'at the expense of' necessary.

So much of leadership strategy is focused on exactly that; strategy. When we consider leadership outside of our own workplace contexts, often there is agreement on how it is actually about building relationships and supporting team members. The trouble that can arise is the moment we step inside the organisational environment, and the stressors that exist, either those glaringly obvious or the kind that slowly erodes away at people, it is typical to divert to an approach that is reliant on skills and decision-making within leadership as the default. The emotional, relational, and strategic aspects of leadership then become fragmented, where strategy itself remains the default and emotional and relational approaches become viewed as either a 'nice to have' or, even less considered, 'unnecessary' to the real functions of success.

We saw this a lot throughout the journey of the COVID-19 pandemic: at the onset, some large organisations that were already heavily espousing values as a part of their appeal went to great lengths to ensure the work-from-home arrangement was supported for every team member. They had their IT teams working overtime, in some cases driving around and delivering computer equipment in a COVID-safe handover to the homes of employees, so that team members could have what they needed to perform their role and so that their client base had as close to uninterrupted support and services as could be managed. They went all out, including a variety of stress-support sessions delivered online for each of their departments, acknowledging that 2020, and into 2021, was a globally stressful period of time, filled with uncertainty. All in all, considering the quick response the entire pandemic situation required of businesses, these organisations performed well particularly here in Australia.

Where it fell short was the way in which some organisations chose to continue once restrictions began to ease. Where they once espoused staff safety, providing free annual flu vaccinations for those who wanted them, having temperature checks in the foyer in order to reduce the risk of sharing illness with other co-workers, many of whom statistically were immunocompromised, and having experienced how the business still financially thrived throughout the mandatory work-from-home period for staff members, once restrictions looked like they had started to ease for good, the divestment almost immediately began.

A bit like a slingshot effect, it was as if the entire organisation itself had a stress response that had them contract and then revert, in some cases to less accommodating conditions than prior to the pandemic. But of course, while organisations are their own version of an entity, it is not organisations that make a decision, but the humans involved within them. It was as if the stretch of accommodating change, no matter how successful they had remained and even grown throughout that change, was too much. Before, they were standing straight and tall, the pandemic making them stretch, where you might visually imagine a human standing and stretching their arms and legs out, a bit like Leonardo da Vinci's Vitruvian man, and then instead of exploring that space they have stretched into, or even just dropping their arms and coming back to the neutral they began in, which would have been a much simpler approach, they contracted and curled up into a ball instead. When the stakes were high and when the sudden onset emotional demand started to subside, they forgot all of their progress, even though it looked different to how they might '*have always done things*', and essentially reacted. They let the pendulum swing not back just to the middle, but a little further away in the opposite direction, negating their efforts and progress, and negatively impacting everyone who was benefiting from it.

It is so human to sit on that pendulum even a little, but in the many cases in which this happened all over the globe, it impacted the even more humans within those organisations. Their leaders were not showing up with mindful consideration of the true impact, or with the emotional intelligence that recognised how this contraction might feel for their employees; it was simply a defaulting – further – back to pre-existing ways of decision-making that, particularly in the face of the global changes that had occurred as a result of the global pandemic, almost make a lot of these ways of decision-making obsolete. But perhaps this in itself was an emotional response; the need for familiarity and the illusion of stability to create that further illusion of control. Except this time it was at the expense of their team, how they felt, and the culture that was created as a result.

When the stakes feel high, everything is fast moving or emotionally demanding, and we are back in the regular swing of things in the workplace while navigating hybrid or global teams, how you show up emotionally as a leader is just as important as what you decide in your leadership position. Leadership becomes performative when there is the display of emotional intelligence without the true practice of presence it requires. And when leaders focus solely on mindfulness without applying it to how they interact with the world around them – without emotional intelligence – they risk putting their focus on so much inwardly in attempts at 'hacking' their way to growth that they are either detached from those around them, or end up bypassing, spiritually or within their leadership role, at the attempt to continue mindfulness in a way that only serves them.

Mindfulness itself is a really important tool and practice, with a great many benefits that are core to your personal wellbeing. However, when you leave it there, you leave short-handed. It becomes only about you, how *you* feel, and how *you* experience the world. Even outside of leadership, this centring of your self becomes an issue when you try to develop relationships of any kind. In leadership, missing out on the key second part of this work can mean not fulfilling your role as effectively as you can.

Leaders are not solely moved up the ranks because they are so good at the technical skills of their given profession. That may be a part of what gets you recognised, but moving into leadership roles – or continuing in them – requires a whole additional skill set that becomes even more important for you to develop now that you exist in that role. Without the development of emotional intelligence as a skill, and continually practising that however imperfectly, mindfulness alone is a fragmented approach that will not serve you or your success as much per your efforts.

It is by unifying these practices that leaders like you can access more authentic connection, a clearer perception of people and circumstances around you, and more effective, values-aligned decision-making and actions.

The Congruence Between Head, Connection, and Presence

Goleman's EI model and Jon Kabat-Zinn's mindfulness work, amongst contemplative neuroscience and different leadership agility theories certainly lend their hand at developing foundations around congruence. These foundations allow leaders to thrive rather than just surviving or 'getting by'. They do so by encouraging us as leaders to lead as a whole person, rather than splitting our attention and investment on either people *or* performance. It is people *and* performance, in this case.

In yoga, we talk about it as the connection between your head, heart, and body. Your head being the still very important aspect of cognitive clarity, where you make and are aware of decisions, and your conscious centre of ethics and thought processes. Your heart being your connection with self enabling your connection with others. How you empathise, your social intelligence, your care and the actions that support your values. Your body is your centre for presence, your awareness of yourself, your tone, how you show up. It's also your regulation of yourself, and the intentionality in which you exist, beyond just a presentation of yourself and more as *you*. It's more about how you are *being* than how you are just *doing*.

Hardly a new concept overall, this congruence between head, heart, and presence in leadership is still relatively undervalued in the professional, more corporate world. When we are more collectively able to remove it from the list of 'nice to have but we're not investing in that right now' to a comprehension of how valuable and key it is to the function of leadership, and therefore business success, that it is, more leaders, employees, teams, and organisations will be able to thrive at a higher standard, with more relative ease. This framework and approach as a core function of business, similar in the way that accounting and legal alignment are, is the next evolution that accounts for the very real human experience of existing, including the body, nervous system, complexity of relationships, and post-pandemic and global events fatigue in leadership.

We get to explore not only why this approach in practice is valuable, but also *how* you as a leader or member of a team can practise your own head, heart, and presence in your career.

2 Mindfulness and Presence as Your Foundation

It can be hard to know where to start when you look at the breadth of work that is mindfulness, emotional intelligence, even leadership itself. Some of these ideas can feel challenging to deconstruct into attainable or achievable moments. When I'm looking at a complicated project, with a lot of different pieces that could, arguably, go in any which order, I remind myself of this: Sometimes the best way to start is to pick a spot and start.

Something happens for your brain and your energy in that moment as well. The barrier to getting started is dissolved, and while the work itself continues and may have its own complexities, that 'blank page, void of direction' feeling can't exist because you have simply started.

Consider this section the laying of your foundations to where to start, and let it be simple.

Mindfulness in Leadership: What and Why?

In order to apply mindfulness in leadership, you could consider mindfulness through two main approaches in a practical sense. One is mindfulness as engagement, which pays more active attention to your levels of awareness and your relationship with your experiences. Through more engagement with your thoughts or feelings that are showing up in the present moment, it allows you to facilitate a deeper understanding and interaction with your environment around you. The other is approaching mindfulness as relief. This approach focuses on utilising mindfulness techniques and practices to support stress reduction or even encourage states of relaxation or contentment (Choi et al., 2021).

With both of these approaches, ways that mindfulness can show up in a practical application are through presence. Practices of presence are those that train you to pay attention to what is happening right now. As useful as reflection is, it can become detrimental when it shifts into ruminating on the past. Similarly, regarding the future; creating a vision to work towards is a necessary part of leadership, but when your relationship to that vision is fostering increased anxiety or dread, perhaps in concern that it may never happen, or that you're 'not there yet', you have stepped out of the realm of usefulness as a leader in that moment and in that sense of vision.

DOI: 10.4324/9781003632771-3

Practising presence is more about noticing what is happening, showing up, or apparent in real time. It is a bit like noticing the feeling of the soles of your feet connecting with the ground as you walk, the feeling of the steering wheel underneath your hands, or catching when your shoulders are cosplaying as earrings. Noticing this means that you can help those shoulders to release that tension by dropping them back down, because you are now aware of it. This is how practices of presence benefit leadership the most significantly. When you can notice circumstances as they arise in any given moment, you can then respond to them in a more effective and timely way.

When a leader of any kind – whether a manager, a high-ranking official, a business owner, or any title – stops paying attention to the present because they are so caught up in rumination on the past, or heightened anxieties about the future, they miss the opportunities to respond to and mitigate circumstances as they arise *in the moment*. For example, consider anxieties around money and cash flow. A manager might be so worried about what is coming next, or be dealing with their own higher-ups' pressures of money already spent, that they forget to plan for expenses happening today; but missing that bill today means the service provider is shutting it off, rendering useless the manager or their team's ability to carry out their business, and maybe even their ability to bring in more cash to flow.

Each of these things is necessary – reflection, anticipation, and presence – to an extent, but losing out on the present moment effectively complicates things. In a more people-management example: a leader is caught up in previous mistakes a member of their team has made. Perhaps they are even working themselves up about it, even though it has been addressed and rectified. They might project an idea of how this team member will handle a future project coming up, where the manager tries to over-control and micro-manage the situation and the entire team. What they then do not notice, because they are busy letting their attention only be on the past mistake, and in the future projection, is the confusion they are causing with the current client. This manager's worry, and subsequent involvement in tasks that are assigned to the responsibilities of others, has left the client confused because they now have more than one point of contact and have received differing information. This also leads to gaps in communication with the client, when more than one person is attempting ownership over the account so emails are getting missed. This naturally impacts the client's experience, and potentially the end product or finished outcome. In this scenario, the manager is still not noticing because instead of managing their team, they are leading with stress.

It is important to remember that when we talk about mindfulness in leadership, and how good it is for the team of people who work with and around these leaders, there is always an end goal. Team members' quality of experience *is* important and should be prioritised. Just as much as remembering that how things operate internally will always reflect, if not impact directly, externally. Whether you have direct customers, clients, or external stakeholders, the 'end client' is at risk of experiencing the outcomes of distracted, unmindful, or mindless leadership. In order for your business or organisational success to be a priority, so must your people, and yours and their experiences, be a priority as well. Too many leaders think they are leading well by only using the metric of customer satisfaction, forgetting that customer experience is informed by their experience with the people of that organisation – and since we are all human, that can vary depending on the quality of the environment internally. Organisations that have high levels of internal stress, particularly when that stress is caused or at the very least not helped by leadership, have less capacity to serve their clients or customers in a way that feels both fulfilling for the team members and satisfying for the end customer. What your customers are experiencing externally is most often a reflection of the environment and culture internally. Sir Richard Branson once said,

> Take Care of Your Employees, and They Will Take Care of Your Business

The most important thing to remember is to take this quote off your shelf of motivating one-liners and put it into meaningful practice so that it can actually serve you meaningfully.

The Simplicity and Complication of Practicing Presence

Mindfulness through the practice of presence means being aware of your thoughts, feelings, sensations, and surroundings without trying to resolve anything or creating stories about or judging them. It is simple in concept, but often challenging in practice. So why should you bother?

When you are in a busy workplace, or busy yourself either building your career, running a business, or leading teams while trying to perform all of the other demands upon you, it is easy to de-prioritise the things that you cannot measure the value or return on investment of on a spreadsheet. Often, and unfortunately for both you and your people, mindfulness practices fall into the category of 'unimportant'.

These skills can come into play both inside and outside of the workplace, often in the most unexpected of moments.

I have spent years diligently renewing my First Aid and CPR qualifications annually, as required for insurance purposes and also peace of mind, just for the sake of being prepared to use those skills should I need to – mostly unexpectedly. There are countless times I recall having to sit in the training room, or some basement-style room of some pub where the training was held, wondering why I had to spend a day of my precious time doing this *again* when 'I already know how to bandage and do chest compressions'. Or feeling silly in the role play moments where we had to pretend to go through our DRSABCDs (the formula to check Danger, Response, Send for Help, Airway, Breathing, CPR, and Defibrillation that Australian certified First Aid Courses teach) for the assessor, trying to show that I was taking their work seriously while also trying not to put on my best drama-student method during the 'Call Triple Zero!' call out.

It was the same every year, but I showed up. Firstly, because I had to if I wanted my insurance to be worth anything, and secondly, despite everything else, I am nothing if not a planner and situational preparer. I showed up and paid attention because I understand the importance of practice and reminding ourselves of a process through repetition so that if, and when, something happened that called upon these skills, it was far easier for my instincts to follow in the most helpful direction. Making it therefore far easier for me to follow those instincts. Practising the moment long before I even knew I might need it. It was brain and energy efficiency – which is exactly what happened the day I witnessed a road accident where people were injured.

I was not driving, which put me in the perfect position to – following an instinct rather than a conscious thought or decision – get myself out of the car door as it was still coming to a stop, phone in hand dialling emergency services. I call this an instinct because I wasn't sitting back first and thinking my way through all the things to do. I simply did them, and I call them a trained instinct because I had, more or less, practised that exact moment, even without the scenario, every year for about 13 years at that point. I could get a hold of emergency services, while other bystanders were the ones who rushed to attend to the people involved and support that side of things. I could communicate clearly, even with my shaky voice, between the dispatcher and the support people right there in front of me. It is something that I have genuinely felt grateful for every day I have thought of it since. Not because there was a lack of other people around who could have done that part just as much – there were so many people ready to help in that moment – but because I could actually contribute usefully.

The second lesson during that event showed up in how I noticed myself responding to it in the present moment. Because I teach mindfulness and, as a result, have gone over this theoretical stress response uncountable times prior, it became a very simple process for holding myself through the stress response in the moment – and for dealing with the aftermath, which I will get to shortly. This is also important in a First Aid scenario so that I didn't become an additional burden on the situation. If I am overcome in the moment, I am not helpful to anyone in the situation that I have stepped up to be in.

I noticed that my voice was shaky. Shaky in the way that only a dump of stress hormones in your system would make it. Adrenaline has this wonderful effect of making everything clearer and focused to help you move through the shock, but it doesn't happen unnoticed. For me, it was a strong body, steady breath, and shaky voice; understandably so, considering the circumstances. I remember naming this to the Triple Zero dispatcher. I wanted to ensure she knew I was clear-headed, there was no confusion, but that my voice was telling on me of the shock of it all. Naming it even helped me manage it.

At some point, my job was to just remain on the call with the dispatcher until the critical care ambulance team arrived. There was not much else for me to do as we waited. Knowing myself well enough to know that I apparently do better in a crisis when I have a job to do, I appointed little jobs to myself. I first took the opportunity to ground myself. So I walked back to the car, which was still where we had stopped, and used the opportunity to take a few deep breaths. I mustered the slowest exhales I could without making myself feel panicky on the other side of it. It was a gentle approach. Unforced, without expectation other than just breathing for a moment. After four or five breaths, I felt a bit steadier to go back and check in on the injured and the people supporting the injured. This continued even once I was off the phone again.

Having the awareness during a stressful event that I could not magically make the event go away, I knew I had to hold myself through it in ways while it was happening in order to be more of a support. This importance and seriousness in the situation was what kept me focused. But what happens after the big event? After the big adrenaline dump that throws your body into big stress? That particular day I had been heading back to an old apartment to clean it before picking up my dog. She had been staying at a friend's place while we had been moving house for the week. I was offered the option to just go straight to the dog and sort the cleaning out another day. Again, this is where my practice kicked in for me.

Amelia Nagoski (2025) talks about the stress cycle being a physiological response to perceived threats, which follows a specific process to 'complete' the stress cycle in order to avoid or prevent burnout. It presents stress almost visually as a tunnel, where we move through the tunnel as part of the completion of the stress cycle in order to reach a state of relief, or ease. If we don't, it risks us becoming 'stuck' in the tunnel, which can lead to burnout. Fortunately for timing, I had been reading Amelia and her sister Emily's book 'Burnout' just prior to this event. Most importantly, I remembered the main thing they found helped individuals like me in that moment, to complete the stress cycle. The top of the list? Physical activity. While spiritually it was the last thing I wanted to do in the moment once everything was cleared, people had been taken to hospital, police had been spoken to, and we could be on our way, I remembered this: that engaging in exercise or movement is found to be the most effective way to help release pent-up stress, and complete that so-called stress cycle.

Having been teaching mindfulness and stress awareness for years at that point already, I was fortunate to recognise the signs of stress in my body – beyond the glaringly obvious point that an event like that would of course naturally cause a stress response. I had started to feel that turn of the stress injection; the shift that would eventually result in the slump, leading to fatigue after the event. Knowing what I had already learned, having practised it, and learning these newer things prior to this particular stress event equipped me with the ability to recognise it, remember that fun fact about physical activity, and make the decision that would support me processing it as best as possible. We went and cleaned the apartment.

Fortunately, two of the other methods Nagoski talks about that help to signal safety in the body after a stress response were social connections, which I got with my safe people when picking up the dog, and sleep, which was ultimately inevitable after a day like that. Conveniently for the purposes of this book and story, practising mindfulness was also on the list; useful for enhancing awareness which allows us to better manage stress responses.

Because if we are not aware of it, we cannot make decisions in support of it. If I was not previously informed of the stress response, or practised just enough in mindfulness to notice the telltale signs showing up in my body during and after the event, how was I meant to be *able* to make decisions to support myself through it? How was I meant to be *able* to give myself what I needed, sooner to when I needed it, for my overall wellbeing?

Proactive Wellbeing and Where Divestment Happens

The first half of 2020 saw a great influx in implementing wellbeing-centric measures within organisations. Brought on by the necessity of a global, pandemic-caused lockdown, organisations had to follow suit. While there are plentiful examples of organisations that either did not do this well or tried the most to sneak ways around it, there were many more that suddenly showed their aptitude for being able to enact measures and programmes in order to support their people – whether those people were working from home or had to remain to work on location. COVID-19, while globally disastrous in many ways, was also a conduit to a different way of operating in business. Gears were swiftly shifted, IT teams worked overtime to make it work for everyone, and mindfulness as a form of personnel support was bumped up high on the priority list by board directives. During what was collectively a deeply challenging time, from a wellbeing perspective, there seemed to be a small light at the end of the tunnel. A light that suggested we may just be entering a new era of how we approach and prioritise wellbeing at work, even beyond the initial instigator of a global pandemic.

Then consider how many of those organisations swiftly divested from those measures, the further away from lockdown that we all got. Over the six years since, companies have continued to roll back these measures in an attempt to 'get things back to the way they were'. Boards, who showed such promise in their seemingly people-first priorities, reacted perhaps out of fear of an uncertain economic environment or the desire to return to what's comfortable and measurable in the ways they recognise. They went from 'let's do everything we can to invest in support for our people' to ignoring all of the fresh research coming out about things like working conditions that suggested flexible arrangements were more economically beneficial for both company and employee, not least to mention the dismissal of all of the wellbeing benefits they experienced by supporting their people with a variety of mindfulness initiatives we all saw rolled out. They divested from those measures in a way that makes March of 2020 feel even longer ago than the calendar suggests.

This divestment feels to me much like the decision not to renew your CPR for the third year running because you 'know enough already'. Then, when it comes time to actually needing to step into action, you freeze because you haven't practiced it recently. Or the decision to put off filing your tax return because you're simply 'too busy', only to find yourself five years down the track desperately backtracking to avoid getting into further trouble; perceiving it to be much simpler just by doing what you need to at the time it is needed, rather than preparing for or mitigating the trouble it might cause you by operating in this way.

Mindfulness practices are the same, or at least similar – better and far more effective when we practise them regularly *before* we actually need them. It is much harder to access the practise when our brains are already in a state of stress. Not impossible, but certainly more challenging. And that's if you even remember it. When our brains are in a state of stress, the logical centres are not as engaged, so it is naturally harder to think up new information that you have never learned before. Memory itself is even challenged, but your body and brain can rely a little bit more on developed neural pathways; those patterns that help us follow something we have already done before. It is why we will sometimes arrive home not remembering the drive in the car at all; suddenly worrying how it is you didn't do anything illegal, or got there in one piece, because you knew the pattern of how to get home so your brain did not need to think as hard to get you there. It just knew where to turn, that it needed to stop at red lights and go at green lights, and how to accelerate and brake. It was a practised pattern. The more you practise doing something, the more second nature it becomes. It is also why it can take a bit to get used to driving a new car, where the indicator stalk is on the other side of the steering wheel. Our natural habits create the path of least resistance and the most efficiency for our brains.

Many organisations have either divested from wellbeing support or simply do not see it as a priority they are focusing on right now because they misunderstand the benefits. In a study by Osgood et al. (2024), it explored the effects of cognitive appraisal, an adaptive emotion regulation method, on mental health symptoms. While the study was on active-duty military personnel who had completed overseas deployment in the previous 18 months, the results lead to an interesting outcome that could be applied to anyone feeling adversely affected by their own experience of high stress at work. Stress is not the same as mental illness, but mental illnesses and conditions such as post-traumatic stress disorder (PTSD) can be exacerbated by stress. Overall, the study found that cognitive reappraisal helps mitigate the effects of combat exposure on mental health.

The practice of cognitive reappraisal is a form of antecedent-focused emotion regulation, where through focused mindfulness practices, participants reframe their thoughts and stories they have about stressful experiences in order to reduce the level of perceived emotional distress they associate with that experience. This strategy can lead to lower levels of anxiety, enabling individuals to interpret their experiences in a more manageable way, and is associated with various positive mental health outcomes. Individuals are more enabled to maintain a more balanced emotional state; in the case of this study, it was post-combat, which has the potential to foster better coping strategies, resilience, and lower severity of symptoms like PTSD and anxiety. While I am in no way comparing combat warfare to just another day in the office, it could be assumed that if some mindfulness practices have been shown to be effective for arguably more extreme cases and causes of stress, they could be useful for our more everyday kinds of stress.

Mindfulness practices, such as cognitive reappraisal as found in this study, are associated with various positive mental health outcomes, enabling individuals to experience more emotional balance, develop better coping strategies to stress, and cultivate real resilience – not just the forced type that is all talk, and mostly dysregulation. When mindfulness is practised by leaders, you develop your own ability to navigate dysregulation, and manage your stress in healthier ways. Mindfulness does not make stress and stressors magically go away, but it can help to make the larger waves of the experience feel a little smaller and more surmountable, with less energetic, mental, or emotional effort to do so. When leaders show up in that way in their organisations, and help to proactively cultivate a culture of practices that their team members can learn, experience, and benefit from, they are leading companies that are more resilient, and tend to feel better about it in the process.

The Cognitive Benefits of Staying Present

As with any methodology to do with the body or the mind, there are things we can do that make us feel good (or at least better), things we can do that make a tangible difference, and things we can do that offer us both. It can be challenging to know the difference between the things that make us feel good and the things that make an actual difference. Just like there is a challenge in finding or accessing those methodologies that make a difference and choosing to work through the potential discomfort, even if they do not immediately feel 'good'. Our brain will always want that immediate reward, so knowing what supports us, even if there is delayed gratification on the way there, is part of the practice.

It is becoming ever-increasingly important to not only explore the options you have available, both personally and professionally, but to also better understand those options, particularly in relation to what you are looking for. If you are looking for something that just makes you feel good, that does not make you wrong. It's a judgement-free zone. But you may need to adjust your expectations on the results it provides. If you are looking for a methodology that makes a difference, it's helpful to understand the distinction between those methodologies that are effective but not always 'good' feeling, and those that have the potential of giving you a bit of both.

Then there is the consideration that each person's experience will be different. Just like you cannot prescribe the exact same workout to everyone in the world and expect everyone to love it or get the most out of it, you cannot approach mindfulness with the expectations of same-same-same: same approach —> will equal same experience —> will equal same benefits. This could be why mindfulness, particularly as it relates to wellbeing, can be such an overwhelming and uncertain topic to approach. As a professional, you're naturally busy focusing on your own career interests, your own craft. Fortunately, there are ways we can begin to understand the impact of mindfulness practices within the workplace to help direct leaders.

In a study from 2024 by Awan et al., responses from 311 individuals across various individuals working in R&D (research and distribution) found that workplaces that embrace mindfulness as a core practice can expect a range of positive outcomes that help to enhance both individual employee performance, as well as overall organisational effectiveness. The cognitive and neurological benefits of mindfulness naturally seem to equate to psychological and behavioural outcomes because of implementing mindfulness practices. In this study's case, it particularly related these outcomes to the creative process engagement.

Improved Attention and Focus

Mindfulness has been found to help improve attention and focus. In the Awan et al. study, practising mindfulness encouraged this by enhancing the capacity of participants to concentrate more clearly on relevant information and reducing attention focused on distractions. Imagine the times when you have been attempting to focus on something, like trying to go to sleep, and all you can hear is the mosquito in the room. Suddenly, in the dark, the mosquito sounds like the loudest thing in existence, and it becomes all you can focus on. This outcome suggests that mindfulness helps you to focus more on the efforts of going to sleep – perhaps the rhythm of your breath or the heaviness of your body – eventually noticing the mosquito buzz less and less. In a workplace, it could be the sound of other people talking that becomes a distraction, whether they are talking physically near you or keeping the group chat notifications alive and active. Mindfulness helps to train your brain to focus on what is useful and *feel* less distracted by the outside chatter – whether the chatterboxes actually go away or not. You are not necessarily trying to control the behaviour of the people around you. The aim is not to over-control the environment. The aim is helping yourself to adjust what you focus on and how you respond to it.

This is also why I encourage participants in a mindfulness session to practice being OK with distracting noises. As much as I would love to create the perfect bubble for them to experience the practice in – and there are relaxation benefits to those kinds of sessions too – the reality is, real life will always have distractions. When we practise things like mindfulness, in whatever form that practice comes in – be it yoga, meditation, surfing, gardening, nature bathing – only in the perfectly curated moments, with perfectly ideal conditions, do we not actually develop the skill for presence in the same way, if at all. Sea captains will tell you they did not learn to sail rough conditions on smooth seas. Just in the same way you will not learn to develop your skills in presence and focus when you have nothing distracting you. There is a difference between constantly putting yourself in situations that always distract you, so you can never really feel presence, and taking it as it comes if circumstances happen to be that way.

For example, I have taken many groups of soldiers through eight-week mindfulness meditation courses to help them develop these skills in emotion recognition and regulation, mindfulness, presence, and breathwork. The big, basketball court-sized gym we would hold these sessions in echoed a lot, and being the warehouse kind of old-gym structure it was, had little insulation from the outside. There were times after sessions I would chat to participants, and they would mention how loud the crows were. Crows were all they could focus on some sessions, and they lamented they could not relax or get the most out of the session that they thought they should. These were the moments I would remind them of the skill they were building. Yes, I would have loved to have made it a much more comfortable, peaceful environment for them, but the reality is that we were holding these sessions on a Defence base, so outside noises were going to be a part of the norm. Whether it was crows, the sound of basketballs bouncing on the courts behind the gym, the revving of military vehicles driving past, or even people outside shouting out to each other, this was their usual day-to-day environment, so it was also an ideal environment for them to develop this skill in.

I started taking the opportunity at the beginning of each of the sessions to remind them they may hear outside noises. I would remind them that outside noises are OK to hear and even encourage them to let their brain acknowledge its presence. Much like a small child or a hungry cat wanting attention, these kinds of noises only seem to get louder the more we try to ignore them. Participants found that when they gave their mind permission to acknowledge the presence of the sound and even identify what it might come from – without allowing for the mind to get too caught up in trying to solve anything – their mind actually relaxed a little more. Feedback they began giving me after sessions from then was that they were able to not notice the noise as much the further we got into the practice and found it easier to keep focused on the guided meditation and their experience instead.

During a body rotation exercise, they were more easily able to be present to the sensations in their body just by beginning the practice with this reminder and acknowledgement. This is a skill that might have taken them longer to develop if the physical environment were what we would otherwise call 'perfect'. All I needed to do beyond that was occasionally quietly request that other people in the building lower their voices. This was more to do with the situational awareness of how the participants might naturally feel more alert when hearing loud voices, their systems and training attuned to responding and standing to attention with immediacy. While there is always a situational awareness to consider with yourself or with others, and adjustments may be needed, you do yourself a disservice if you let yourself get caught up in expecting to develop these valuable skills within perfection.

When you are trying to control the people and the environment around you, it risks creating more stress in your body and a sense of vigilance that does not serve your attentiveness well. It is important to acknowledge there are circumstances and situations people might experience that would naturally, and understandably, impact their ability to feel physically safe enough to turn their focus more inward. People in countries ravaged by conflict might find their version of presence is drastically different from those of us who are fortunate enough to be secure at home on our couch or in our bed attempting to practise the same. Take this reminder that mindfulness practices, particularly when it comes to attention and focus, are extremely subjective from person to person, and experience to experience, and therefore must be approached as a unique experience with an awareness of what you might be aiming for, but a more relaxed grip on the expectation to allow yourself to have your own experience each time you set down to.

Enhanced Emotional Regulation

Mindfulness practices have also been found to cultivate better emotional management in those who practise it over a longer period of time. This equips participants of mindfulness with a better ability to regulate their responses to things like stress, even when related to carrying out their work tasks, as well as their responses to challenges that arise during creative tasks. It can make the difference between feeling dread about coming up against a challenge during a creative process at work, and actually enjoying the learning experience *even though* it is challenging. More effective emotional regulation helps you to change your relationship with the stressor. There is no requirement for you to always like it; it does not ask you to change your preference. Instead, mindfulness encourages you to develop an element of emotional control that helps you to more effectively problem solve. This emotional control is linked to improved cognitive flexibility. At work, this improved skill in cognitive flexibility can look like having a greater ability to see around the reaction of a particular stressor and explore more of the possibilities available to you. These possibilities are otherwise so much harder to see when you are in the affected state and unable to emotionally regulate. It is important to go in aware of your relationship with dysregulation. We should not see dysregulation itself as the 'bad' thing; it can instead be really informative for your experience and what impacts that experience for you or for others. It is simply something you get to choose to respond to, or not.

Viktor Frankl, an Austrian psychologist and Holocaust survivor, wrote about his experiences in the Nazi concentration camps, including as a prisoner at Auschwitz-Birkenau, the most deadly of the Nazi extermination camps, in his book *Man's Search for Meaning*.

> Everything can be taken from a man but one thing: the last of the human freedoms—to choose one's attitude in any given set of circumstances, to choose one's own way.

It is a reminder of what emotional regulation can allow for us, gifted to us from a survivor of one of the most harrowing mass experiences in modern history. Frankl reminds us in this concept that when we are able to create just enough space between whatever has activated us and how we are immediately reacting, and perceive what this is so we can then consciously decide how we would like to respond to our circumstances, we experience freedom. Even when your immediate reaction might be a perfectly reasonable response to what is occurring, Frankl suggests that you are still caught up in the limited sense of not getting a choice over how your response is acted upon. He, instead, suggests that when you become more aware of your reactions to outside stimuli, you are then better placed to choose what you then actually do about it – your response in 'action'. This is where you empower yourself with the freedom over your choices, versus being the continual victim of your first, immediate emotion. The first emotion has a right to exist; Frankl's perspective just helps us to find practices to choose around it, instead of being at the mercy of it.

This is an advanced level of thinking for someone in such extreme circumstances as he faced during the Holocaust, and perhaps we and the rest of the world were very fortunate that he happened to already be practising in the psychology field prior to his experiences, for him to put that psychology lens of awareness in his explanations for us all. Regular workplaces in areas of the world that are not affected by conflict cannot compare to the experiences of World War II extermination camps, yet there is still a lot we can apply with these deeper awarenesses we are fortunate to learn from those who have shared with us their experiences. Here, the value of not acting on every immediate response you feel to an annoyance, inconvenience, or frustration at work is, arguably, the bare minimum of showing up to work and creating a safe workplace for your peers. Yet, when we practise it, we learn it can go deeper than even immediate reactions. This practice of becoming more attuned and aware of our emotions when something activates them allows people, leaders in particular, to then be more attuned to when those emotions prompt certain decision-making processes.

How many decisions have been made by people in positions of leadership that were, quite clearly, based on an emotional reaction to something else? And how many of them ended up being the most supportive decisions and outcomes, versus how many could have been better for *everyone*, including the business, had the decision been different?

When leaders make decisions, there are three factors to consider: what changes when the decision has been made (including what it no longer allows for), how they are communicating that decision and projected outcome to all the relevant stakeholders, and the impact after the decision is enacted.

In some businesses, the emotional decision may be more of an inconvenience, potentially leading to a lessened stakeholder experience. For example, a fast food manager gets frustrated with the supplier of their salt, so as a reaction decides not to re-order more salt from that supplier in the moment of frustration. The outcome is that they run out of salt for the hot chips, leaving customers feeling less satisfied with their order but ultimately unharmed. This is not ideal and could impact the reputation of that particular store.

In other organisations, the emotional reaction-based decision may have more of a damaging flow-on effect. For instance, a leader of a nation gets too caught up in negative social media posts by citizens and begins making policy decisions based on their embarrassed or ashamed reaction, with a desire to make themselves feel 'right' and like they are the protagonist they imagine themselves to be. The outcome, risking that some of those policy decisions are not the most well thought out, could be harmful to those citizens, their economy, their health, or their communities. It could risk creating more division, which means fewer people are actually working together to improve things, instead spending a lot of taxpayer-covered time on arguments, in-fighting, and filibustering. At best, this helps no one. At worst, history tells us it can cause civil war leading to many deaths.

No matter where you work, the space between the stimulus and the response becomes all the more important when you are working with other people. As a leader, that is quite literally a part of your job description. What is not a part of anybody's job description is a requirement to particularly enjoy everything that does come up, or to ignore their own feelings and experiences completely. You are completely entitled to have your own feelings and reactions to things that you feel affect you. As a leader, it is your responsibility to effectively train yourself to more frequently, even if imperfectly, notice these reactions and use the tools available to navigate them. In doing so, you ensure that you have better foresight on the longer-term impact of your decisions made and actions taken. In addition to that, having the improved ability to emotionally regulate helps to support your experience along the way. A nervous system that is based purely on reaction can feel like an exposed wire; raw, reactive, unable to rest and enjoy much, not to mention the experience of those around. Having the skills to emotionally regulate to some degree helps your workplace experience improve when you are better able to communicate and be more heard and understood. When you are spending most of your time as a leader repeating concepts over to the same sea of blank faces and misunderstandings, it is bound to be frustrating. In being able to communicate more clearly, because you are clearer on your decision even if still having your own emotional experience, everyone – including you and the organisation – benefits more.

It is important to note that, naturally, there are conditions and diagnoses that do require more support from appropriate health professionals. These conditions, such as PTSD and C-PTSD (complex trauma), as well as mental health conditions, are important to keep in mind as you navigate for yourself and for members of your team. Whether you are privy to that information or not – or have a right to that information in your position as a leader or not – it is best to be aware that there may be factors for those around you that you are *not* aware of which play a role in how effective these mindfulness measures are for others, particularly in this area of emotion regulation.

Neurological Changes

There is existing research that suggests mindfulness can lead to changes in your actual brain structure. No longer the realm of pseudoscientific circles, mindfulness practices can lead to changes in your brain associated with attention, emotion regulation, and self-referential processing. These happen in areas such as the prefrontal cortex and the amygdala; the prefrontal cortex typically being the last part of your brain to fully develop by the time you hit your mid-20s or so. Consider your ability – or lack thereof – to emotionally regulate as a toddler. Big feelings feel even bigger when we are not equipped to navigate them, and we typically have no way of knowing how to regulate those big feelings other than the usual – tantrums, tears, and tiny gesticulations. This is why the role of our caregivers is so important, particularly at these young ages. It is our caregivers' – the adults in the room – role to help us to co-regulate. Caregivers play that ever-so-important role in teaching young children to regulate through big emotions, most often done through co-regulation. If we do not learn that adequately enough, or big life stresses occur later on in our lives, we might struggle in the emotion regulation part of our brain. In one way, living through a variety of experiences that test and, potentially, strengthen our skills to reason and regulate is a part of being human. Brains being brains, however, will respond differently from person to person. Then when you add in traumatic events that can have a significant impact on our brains and our systems, there are extra layers to work with here.

There is established research in the mindfulness research field that draws connections between mindfulness practices and certain neurological changes that can help to enhance cognitive functioning and emotional wellbeing in those undertaking the practices. Research by Hölzel et al. (2011) demonstrated that mindfulness meditation can lead to increases in grey matter density in the brain areas related to emotional regulation. Grey matter plays a crucial role in brain function, including being involved in decision-making, problem-solving, and memory functions. Regions with high concentrations of grey matter, such as the prefrontal cortex, are linked to executive functions and complex thinking. Executive functioning in leadership relates to your ability to execute tasks. It is a function that naturally looks different for each person, since each of our brains is very unique from one another. This is where some traditional presentations of executive functioning may not be the norm for some leaders. But when you are supporting your own brain with these mindfulness practices, there can be an improvement in the experience of self-regulation.

In a workplace leadership environment in particular, the evidence of mindfulness practices (Zeidan et al., 2010) being linked to improvements in the executive functioning areas of working memory and cognitive flexibility can only strengthen your ability and effectiveness as a leader. You might have natural leadership abilities already, but if we look socially to the examples of leadership traditionally available to us, not all of them provide great examples of cognitive flexibility. Working memory supports you beyond simply remembering every team member's name, or the exact budget figures for the last five quarters. Working memory also serves for how we learn in leadership, including how we learn from history what not to do. Too many new leaders step into their positions and, in an attempt to prove that they are capable of strong leadership, focus too quickly on making grand, sweeping changes without taking the time to consider why certain systems are in place to begin with. When leaders take the time to use their cognitive functioning – particularly in memory and flexibility – to first understand why previous decisions have been made, even if they are no longer the best decisions, they are better positioned to steer the ship in a more useful direction without destroying the foundations that have already been laid. This also avoids the risk of unnecessary time, money, and morale being spent just for the sake of optics.

Grey matter also helps to process sensory information received from the body. This is important to help you and your brain integrate sensory data more effectively. This further assists you in emotional regulation, particularly in workplace environments – whether online or in the office – where we are exposed to far more sensory input. Changes in grey matter density have also been correlated with learning and memory capabilities, indicating its role in acquiring and retaining information.

In addition to this, another study by Desbordes et al. (2012) found that mindfulness practices may help to enhance activation in certain brain regions, particularly those involved in attention control. As a leader, it is unrealistic to expect yourself to show up perfectly, remember everything exactly as it was, and to never have an emotional moment. As a human, it should be expected that this can occur. The purpose of practising mindfulness for these reasons has little to do with perfection, and more to do with supporting your literal biology so that it can support you better as you attend to your role.

In a study on active-duty military members with PTSD by Polizzi et al. (2024), it was found that there are positive correlations in relation to PTSD severity and the implementation of adaptive emotion regulation methods for participants also undertaking cognitive processing therapy (CPT). It showed that adaptive emotion regulation methods were a useful support structure in the treatment programme. Awan et al'.s study supports this by suggesting that these changes in the brain can enhance cognitive functions and emotional stability. In a workplace or career-building context, these changes are beneficial for creativity; creativity being a necessary function not just for the arts, but for any problem-solving, leadership, people-managing, business-progressing endeavour.

Some neurodivergent experiences, with attention-deficit hyperactivity disorder (ADHD) for example, might struggle with traditional presentations of executive functioning. When entering into these practices, like anything, it is important not to expect an exact presentation of how mindfulness can support you to function. When we can support our brain's unique way of functioning with mindfulness practices, often they might show up in more subtle but just as effective ways. Nothing is the magical, superhero 'spider bite' that changes everything in an instant for you. Leadership, like any other skill, is developed with consistent attention and practice, over time, and a willingness to accept it will forever be affected by your very humanness.

Problem Solving and Idea Generation

Every professional, in every business, has likely experienced – or will experience – the challenge of stagnation at some point in their career. The feeling of plateau, latency and being stuck, where the rigidity of thought and doing the same things over and over again, in the same way repeatedly, brings fresh, new ideas to a screeching halt. Many businesses have succumbed to this experience, with many others idling in the prolonged, perpetual struggle that it can bring with it. The Awan et al. study found that mindfulness allows those practising it to approach challenges with a more open and curious mindset, which encourages divergent thinking. Divergent thinking is a necessity in a leader. Yes, you must stay true to and focused on the vision to steer the ship. At the same time, it is just as important to hone the ability to see more detail in the grey areas that can inform you of anything from changes in market trends to changes within the mood and experiences of your team members. As Ted Lasso would say, 'Be curious, not judgmental'. But it is much easier said than done when you are already well down the path of stress that this stagnancy can cause. Mindfulness practices, particularly when practised with consistency, help you to stretch those cognitive 'muscles' so to speak (they are not muscles), and develop a flexibility that enables you to more easily recognise possibilities, which generates innovative solutions. It can assist your brain to connect the dots a little more creatively and in the less obvious ways than what your mind is recognising, or able to recognise, in that stressed, closed-off state.

Pause and consider for a moment where some of your clearest ideas have come to you. Many people report them as 'shower thoughts', where the mindfulness of letting water run over you feels as if it almost clears the muck figuratively, at the same time as literally, giving you clarity or that lightbulb moment. It is possibly also the reason why many leaders will, consciously or unknowingly, suggest a coffee walk during a meeting – where they chat on their way to the cafe, or do a 'walk and talk' (as Aaron Sorkin showed so well in television shows like *The West Wing* and *The Newsroom*), where participants in those sorts of meetings often report getting through a whole lot more than their standard sit-down meetings, and even feeling more energised afterwards. When I worked internally in corporate, I used to encourage all of my meetings to begin with each person recognising something they are appreciating, or acknowledging as a win for them for the day or the week. It allowed them to pause just long enough to be mindful of what they have achieved. While there is always pushback, and the risk of it feeling like it is 'not enough', it is a way of using mindset work as presence, that helps to open up more recognition for more of these successes, in this case.

This practice of presence in recognition, rather than always focusing on just what has *not* happened yet, gradually skills the mind in a subtle form of presence. As we know, the more we practise something, the easier it becomes to do. I found the more people were getting used to looking for the things to acknowledge – whether they were achievements or little progresses along the way – the more they recognised different dots they could connect. Presence comes in many forms of practise, and can seem mostly abstract or lacking obviousness to participants, particularly earlier on in their practise. When we expect the practise of presence to immediately show up as results, we place conditions on the practise that ultimately takes us out of presence itself. So while it may not feel like the most immediately rewarding practise, the point and benefits lie in the practise itself, not the expectation.

Stress Reduction

Different mindfulness and presence practices can help to decrease stress levels and experiences of anxiety. While there is a version of intensity that helps us get into a flow state where we can perform and feel in more of a state of pure performance, chronic stress itself can feel and be depleting to our energy and wellbeing. It is important to consider that people will have different stress thresholds and uses in this area; what feels like 'flow' to one person could feel like boredom or, alternatively, overwhelm, for another. Mindfulness can help participants to decrease some symptoms and feelings of the stress and anxiety that do not feel optimal, which then allows us to have clearer thought processes and enjoy improved cognitive function.

Have you ever wondered why so many people seem to come back from their holiday break ready to either quit their job or transition into a new role or promotion? These breaks are where people get the opportunity to relax a bit more, have more time to themselves and with their families, and to effectively reconnect with their lives. Assuming it is a break that is intended for more relaxation than the many other reasons one might choose a break for, they have stepped away from the typical stressors that layer on day-to-day. As a result, they have been able to gain clarity about what they really want to experience – whether that is in their personal lives or their professional career. Because of this, the post-festive season break is commonly known as a time in recruitment when many people in professional services are typically more open to exploring other options if they feel these newly realised needs are not being met or matched in their current role.

This stress reduction is not just about people quitting their jobs en masse. Having tools that help you manage, and even reduce, your stress can also help you advance in your job, your career, or your business. Using mindfulness provides a clearer view on how to engage in complex tasks more creatively. Sometimes that 'complex task' is simply managing and leading people more effectively, with clearer communication.

Many leaders know the feeling of struggle in communicating with their team in a way that they understand, that feels useful for their energy as a leader, and in a way that also yields the desired results.

Many leaders know the feeling of speaking to a brick wall, just like many team members know that same feeling in return.

It does not mean that the other person is dense and incapable; most often the opposite is true. It can simply be an indicator that something is impeding the coherence necessary for the information and message to transfer from brain to brain, via the spoken word. Many people want the solution to be knowing what to say, so they can replicate it word for word. This only works in some cases, but other times clarity is not so much in exactly what is *said*. Clarity comes in what is *understood*. It is much like me walking into a room full of soldiers and saying 'Now we're going to practice mindfulness'. It seems clear to me – most likely in large part because it is my literal job to know it – but when the word 'mindfulness' has not been a part of that person's particular training or lexicon, it gets lost in translation. Then imagine you are layering stress on top of that conversation. The other person is stressed, in this case, about an injury that is causing chronic pain, and therefore chronic distraction. They are concerned for their career moving forward, or about a relationship in their personal life. They might even be bored. And the person delivering the information might feel stressed because they only know *these* words to tell, and cannot understand why someone else is not understanding. They might feel stressed from the worry this interaction is causing about their ability to actually do this work. 'Maybe I'm not fit to lead' crosses their mind. In any kind of workplace scenario, this is just one example of how stress can compound against how we communicate with others.

When we feel clearer mentally, it is much easier to communicate clearly to the people around us. When we have clearer communication with the people around us, everyone can understand better. It creates a path for everyone to follow. This is all to say that when you lead yourself and take care of your stress, it can serve more people than just you, even if tending to your stress feels like the most selfish thing to do in the moment.

The business itself also gets to benefit from an overall reduction in stress experienced by their people, at any level of role. Nobody wants to walk into a workplace – even virtually logging in – where the air is thick with tension, people are snapping at each other, assuming negative intent in the tone of words used via email where tone is harder to determine by its very nature, and reacting as a result of those assumptions. These workplaces where people are actively choosing not to clarify their understanding of something another has said or done, because they are so caught up in their own stress they forget that the humans around them are also just as equally fallible humans, are harmful for presenteeism and retention. Whether something directly created the issue causing the stress within the business itself, or something more personal outside of the business, not addressing it is linked to more employee absenteeism, illness, fatigue, loss of productivity, and staff turnover. Whether you or your business caused these things, it remains an expensive issue we are then left to deal with.

The most important thing to consider here is even if you are unsure if the cause of the stress is your doing, it still becomes your responsibility to deal with. Not to mention the exhausting, presumably unenjoyable culture it would create. Stress does not get reduced by simply telling yourself or your team members that they 'don't need to feel stressed about' a thing. It gets reduced by enabling people with the tools in a supportive system of processes. The systems in which we exist are what need addressing at the core, not just the fire-fighting materials we give to staff members to deal with.

Collaborative Engagement

Arguably one of the most commonly touted reasons against remote, or even hybrid, work is the fear that teams would lose the benefits of collaborating around the office. While the soundness of this argument would certainly depend on circumstances from industry to industry, and workplace to workplace, there are effective ways to help support a collaborative team environment that more easily engages with each other. Mindfulness practices can help to enhance interpersonal dynamics within teams. This is in part contributed to through the previously mentioned benefits of mindfulness; when stress reduces, people have more capacity to engage with others in a more effective and enjoyable way. When the dynamics of the culture between team members improve, there is a freer, more natural flow of information sharing and collaboration around that information. This free flow of person-to-person engagement supports the cultivation of a healthier workplace culture. It also enriches the collective cognitive resources available that allow for more creativity, more ease in problem solving, more clarity, drive and direction towards the bigger visions.

When we implement mindfulness into workplaces and teams, who then experience the benefits of the stress reduction that can come with practices such as these, it also opens up communication within the team itself. When each person is more aware of their own stress, including how that shows up and what that presents like across different scenarios, their mindfulness practice also helps them to gain clarity on what they need for themselves in those moments. When team members are more aware of when they are stressed in addition to also knowing what they need, it becomes easier for them to communicate that with their teammates. Workplaces that implement mindfulness open up that line of communication and shared language with each other, simply through the awareness function of the practice itself.

When teams of people all contribute to that shared language, they are better able to understand each other. This includes understanding more often when to not take things personally, how to share these experiences and needs better in real time in a way that each person has a more native understanding of, and how to better support each other when others' stress might be high. Practising mindfulness benefits the individual, but it is important to remember that it is also an important part of connecting with, contributing to, and receiving support from community. Even when that community is in the workplace. Building this community mindfully, even when the main goal may be more financial in scope, contributes to more life and work satisfaction for each person. It also contributes to how effectively a team works together. Leaders can support this by leading mindfully, being aware of their own inner world of reactions and responses. You can also support this as a leader by normalising this and encouraging this in your team too.

No person is an island. This applies equally at work. Within the workplace ecosystem, each person's role is there, and should be there, to be a part of a greater whole. Each person's role in the ecosystem of a business helps to support the greater efforts of the business overall by helping to support each role. When leaders, especially aspiring leaders, get caught up in trying to do it all themselves, it damages the business overall. Whether that is through a desire to be the best above and at the expense of all else, or because of a lack of delegation skills they still need to develop, leaders risk failing in their inherent role. This behaviour risks damaging the workplace environment and the potential success of the business outcomes. Collaborative engagement within a team is a priority for successful businesses; therefore, things that enable more of that collaborative engagement must then be just as much of a priority.

Mindfulness can enhance these interpersonal collaboration and sharing dynamics within teams, which ultimately enriches the collective cognitive resources available for more creativity – which also means more problem solving and mitigation along the way.

Mindfulness in Action: Real-World Applications

Practicing mindfulness in leadership looks a lot like the practice of being present with the circumstances that are showing up in that moment. This seems simple, and perhaps even obvious, until you consider what leadership tends to require – or demand – of leaders. Often leaders are primed to look forward into the future in order to anticipate and expect, and therefore mitigate, problems that may arise, or opportunities to lead the vision towards growth. Or they are required to have the skills to reflect backwards on events, trends, or experiences, in order to help their people or their business learn from former mistakes, lest they be repeated again. Both of these are necessary in leadership.

The ability to have a vision for the future and support an organisation, and its people, to move towards it is key to overall success for a leader. It is what leaders are ultimately judged on, and a metric that helps determine your value as a leader regarding increasing your pay rate or even developing your career as you apply to move into new roles. Sometimes, positive judgement is rarely afforded unless they lead that advocacy for themselves.

The future vision for an organisation is a macro view of the overall mission. This is the vantage point from which all other decisions are made in support of that vision. It acts as a rudder for both the business and its people, giving them the direction in which they are moving. It is like having a pilot in the plane's cockpit. They can take a look at all the radars and instruments in order to assess whether they are on track, and have that literal front seat to assess what is ahead in the near future to then determine what decisions need to be made from then. They trust that, as leaders, they can get the plane off the runway and into the air, heading in the direction they need. This trust involves knowing that there is never just one setting of direction, with no adjustments over the course of the journey. These leaders know that once the plane is in the area heading in that general direction, for it to land in the correct place at the goal destination, many check-ins and micro (or major) adjustments are going to be needed along the way. They understand that direction and adjustment-making is their role because they have the tools available in front of them and, even more importantly, know how to use them. The pilot then relays the information to the other team members in the plane so they can do their job most effectively. In this analogy, mindfulness plays the role of air traffic control. It helps them to understand with more clarity what they cannot perceive with their own eyes, so they are better able to make important decisions; decisions which, sometimes, are literally life-saving. Most times, it can ensure it is as smooth an experience as possible for those they serve.

That is the vision for the future and the direction.

Many leaders have erred in mistaking the 'vision' for the 'how' regarding getting to the desired place or outcome. The vision does not, and cannot, suit this purpose. It might inform how you make decisions around the action steps of the 'how', but it cannot be a stand-in for the 'how' alone. A vision alone does not provide the steps for your people to walk upon to get there.

How would a vision help prepare yourself or your people to get through what will show up along the way? It does not build or cultivate the tools for them to navigate that path and all of its obstacles. Without the rewards and acknowledgements of progress along the way, focusing on the vision only risks losing motivation and drive or, at worst, feeding burnout. This kind of burnout occurs when you are so focused on a vision or goal that you forget to acknowledge the moments of progress – whether yours or someone else's – that are getting you there step by step. It is like being the pilot in the plane. Without checking on your instruments to give you regular updates on your direction, you are losing the opportunity to adjust along the way. This 'how' of adjusting along the way would give you the achievement of reaching time and distance milestones as expected. The alternative would more likely be creating more work and energy, or flight time and fuel, than required because you were so busy on only the vision, without checking in along the way. You were so busy just flying that you weren't paying attention to matching that action of flying with the direction of the vision. You lose sight of not only the work required to get there, but acknowledging that work, which is just as valuable too. When you lose sight of how much work you have already done and accomplished in that direction so far, you risk you or your team feeling more lost. It is a quick achievement in demoralisation.

It is not just leaders who are impacted by the lack of acknowledgement. Your team members often go through their own process because of this. They have a manager, in this case you, who should be leading them. But instead, that leader is so focused on the vision that the team's progress along the way, including their hard work each and every day, is going unnoticed. Instead, they are only getting the acknowledgement, and feeling of acknowledgement, when they reach the bigger goal. Not along the way. The problem with this is that goal could be years in the making. This could be years before we even acknowledge all the work required, let alone praised.

In this theoretical scenario, that could look like years of potential overwork and pressure just to bring that ultimate goal closer; overwork that impacts health and productivity outcomes, including but not limited to quality of life and work satisfaction. Unsatisfied team members are not what you are looking to cultivate as a leader. It would also likely mean years of your team members feeling unappreciated at work. Besides years of feeling like they are constantly behind in their work and progress, so that they are always, and only ever, catching up.

This is a risk that is just as crucial for you to consider for yourself, as it is for you as a leader to consider for your team members. How you alone feel at or about your work is not the only thing that is important. If your team members are experiencing these feelings, it risks the integrity and longevity of your organisational culture. You risk being caught up more in staffing and culture issues, ultimately detracting from the vision you're trying to prioritise. If you, as the leader, are feeling all of this pressure on yourself to keep only the bigger vision at the forefront of everything you do, you risk missing out on the richness of everything you get to experience and learn along the way.

The kind of experience that, pragmatically speaking, is the value you can speak to as a leader. The kind of value that you can speak to in future job interviews, online, or on your CV. You risk missing out on this kind of value and experience that conveys your skills and effectiveness as a leader; what those experiencing, hiring, or engaging you want to know.

Although it might feel cliche to hear, it is also the kind of experience that shapes how you feel about your work, your life, and your overall happiness. Safe to say these are also not the qualities that are typically prioritised as much in the corporate world. That is why it is up to you to take the *lead* down this path, even if it is a lonely one to begin with. This experience of fulfilment in how you get to spend your day-to-day in your chosen vocation helps to ensure that your working career is sustainable. A sustainable career allows you better rest and more personal fulfilment during your time off as well. Having that personal fulfilment helps to enrich your working career, just like having job or work fulfilment helps to enrich your personal life; whatever either of those aspects look like in any season of life and work for you.

Similarly, reflection is a skill that serves in how you move forward. Reflection enforces an importance in understanding what has happened previously. Never do I encourage anyone stepping into any role, or new organisation, to immediately begin to make changes without first understanding why the things that are in place are there to begin with. It is important for every leader to take the time to learn to understand, even if it is something that will eventually change once you do. You cannot make or impact effective change without understanding what purpose existing structures or decisions serve, or have served. The existing structures may be outdated, and it may be that you find out exactly how they are no longer working, but you must first understand why they were implemented before making sweeping change; not after.

Those who have come in with the pressure of creating grand sweeping change, but who have not taken the time – and realistically, also not shown the respect – to understand existing structures, previous decisions, and most importantly reasons for those decisions are not serving in their role the way they think they are. New leaders who come in and only make change, for change's sake, without asking questions, are ultimately optic leaders. These optic leaders are just there for show, and not effect. Optic leaders are less able to genuinely implement valuable structural change, and when they do it is likely they have luckily fallen into it. Your experience as it develops as a leader will probably help you recognise certain circumstances sooner and know which questions will help you gain that understanding, all ultimately assisting you to make those decisions in a quicker fashion. The mistake I urge you to avoid making is to do all the changing – even if it is based on previous experience – with none of the understanding or asking.

It is worth noting too that the skill of reflection is not always on display at the highest levels of leadership; instead, it is seen often as optional, or only something required for when something goes wrong. This display of grand sweeping changes with a lack of reflective understanding could understandably contribute to why it feels less effective as a 'leader' to take enough time to ask the questions first. Compared with the examples that have collectively been set for us, it will naturally feel a little uncomfortable. It is natural to feel concern about whether or not you are being an effective leader. We want to follow the examples of what has already been done because they feel safe and 'normal'. It is my duty to remind you at this point that leadership often requires doing things a little – or a lot – differently than how everyone else has done things before. There is a lot we can learn from many styles and versions of leadership. I would be going against my own advice right here if I suggested blindly following without asking questions or understanding why. At the same time, it is the reminder that as much as you and I might really wish that we could just learn something, so that we can set and forget it, and carry on with business, leadership does not work that way. Nor does mindfulness and emotional intelligence. These skills are exactly that; buildable skills that are ever-evolving, the more experience we achieve and the more we learn. Unfortunately, and yet probably for our greatest benefit, there is no set and forget for these things.

When Prior Practice Shows Up in Real Time

A key aspect of mindfulness and presence in leadership is developing the skill to be present with what is showing up right now: circumstances, reactions, emotions, facts, uncertainties, sensations – any and all of it. This practice allows leaders to respond more readily to either crises that already exist or to mitigate future crises. Presence can also allow them to respond to positive experiences. By creating more neutrality in approaching experiences, presence can assist the individual in finding more ease in choosing the response.

Having practised mindfulness before you think you need it helps you in the moments when you are already deep within it. Our breath is an automatic function of our body. Provided nothing else is blocking it or obstructing it, we do not need to remind our brains or our bodies to breathe, or tell them how to breathe. We simply do. There is no thinking it through for every breath as a need: 'Now OK lungs, remember to inhale, and then breathe it out'. At the same time, it is also a function of the body that can be controlled or manipulated in a way to create a certain state. If you were to shorten your breath, you might create a sense of urgency or even anxiety in your body or mind. It is a heightened state of energy that may be useful, or not, depending on what you want to use it to support. If you were to slow down your breathing to some degree, lengthening your inhales and perhaps making your exhales just slightly longer, you might find it to have a more calming effect if you made sure not to stretch it too far. But the automatic function is still there: how many times reading this paragraph about the breath did you find yourself taking a deeper breath?

When you first start lengthening your breath, a count of four might feel excessive and even stressful. After practising over some time, presuming no other limiting health conditions, you might find four counts begin to feel somewhat easier and more accessible. So then, your usual breath practice stretches more naturally to about a count of six, for example. What didn't feel possible or might have even created feelings of stress trying to force it before can feel more calming with the time and practice.

But while slowing down the breath has all the potential health benefits, how slow you get it to isn't so much the goal. It is more the practice of it where you will find the benefits. Diaphragmatic breathing is the process of breathing in deep towards the bottom of your lungs so that when they expand, they gently press the diaphragm, positioned under the lungs, downwards. As a mindfulness practice, diaphragmatic breathing has been found to contribute positively to the wellbeing and mental health of participants, helping them to cultivate not only awareness of their thoughts and feelings, but more acceptance in the process (Van Agteren et al., 2021). This indicates that diaphragmatic breathing can be useful during moments of heightened stress or emotion, or to help find clarity.

Diaphragmatic breathing, also referred to as 'belly breathing', helps you to expand your lung capacity by training the deeper, fuller breath, but in relation to the wellbeing benefits, it also allows you to get accustomed prior to an event that calls for it. This breathwork becomes more supportive to help you get through a stress event, in the acute moments, as a pre-existing tool, which can then be immensely beneficial to helping you navigate processing in the aftermath of a stressful event. Mindfulness training conducted within United States Marines units that included breathwork training resulted in participants exhibiting significant improvements in the response to stress occurrences. These improvements included significantly faster heart rate and breathing rate recovery post-stress, and also demonstrated lower concentrations of neuropeptide Y, an autonomic nervous system marker (Brewer, 2014). So not only were these improvements felt by the participants but also objectively measured. Overall, these benefits showed that recovery from stress, in this study's case more extreme experiences of stress, greatly improved because of mindfulness activities practised *before* the stress was experienced.

When so much emphasis, particularly in workplace environments, is placed on dealing with stress after it has been reported, this understanding of how mindfulness can behave as an effective preventative on the impacts of stress when practiced proactively has the potential to improve how individuals are able to manage and navigate stressful moments. In turn, this creates the potential to shift how workplace support is structured as a system to proactively reduce the negative impacts of stress experienced. These mindfulness practices are always a preventative, however, and cannot speak to other factors in place within the systems that might be contributing to the stress experienced, that might need to be addressed or reduced otherwise.

The Body Really Did Keep the Score

This phrase made regular in our collective lexicons, *The Body Keeps the Score*, is from Dr Bessel van der Kolk's book and work of the same name. Dr van der Kolk is a trauma researcher and educator, particularly at the pioneering front of defining PTSD as a diagnosis. By this statement, he references that our bodies can hold a 'record' of the traumas, or even on a smaller scale, the unprocessed emotions that we have experienced.

Dr Resmaa Menakem also speaks to trauma that is stored in the body, not just in the mind. As a therapist and trauma specialist, Dr Menakem's groundbreaking work and book *My Grandmother's Hands* explores the physical damage that discrimination and racialised trauma have incurred on Black bodies and families intergenerationally, from the perspective of body-centred psychology.

Just like the body keeps the score for the impactful, significant and traumatic moments that we have experienced, the body may also keep 'the score' for those experiences that are also practised by us more intentionally.

For mindfulness specifically, the first time I really noticed my body keeping track of what was happening around me was approximately a year after I had started teaching yoga. One of the foundations, or limbs of yoga asana – the physical practice – is breathwork and the practice of presence. This is specifically practising being present to the breath and the moment, even in the challenge of a particular pose, stretch, or hold. It is taught that this practice helps us to better handle challenges off the mat, helping us to develop a better ability to breathe through those life moments that might feel similarly intense in different ways. To me, the practice is literally a big, fat, giant metaphor for what happens and how we show up to those challenges off the mat. When we can breathe through intensity or challenge, we are potentially able to be less *in* reaction and more often fast track landing at the response part.

At this point in my life, I had been practising yoga, and this specific emphasis on my practice, for approximately five years, in addition to teaching for the year leading up to this point in time. This big moment all happened when I was sitting in a meeting, around a small boardroom table with about five other people in the room. The owner-director of the company was speaking at the front with a whiteboard, with the rest of us listening. Let's call him Gerard. Gerard was talking about something that had to do with the work I was there doing with them when suddenly I noticed my breathing deepen, and my belly slowly and deliberately expanding in and out with longer inhales and exhales. I remember in the moment thinking it was exactly the way I breathe when I am deliberately practising diaphragmatic breathwork, except in that moment this kind of breathing had not been in my conscious thinking awareness. I had just gone from wondering what point was being made at the front of the room to my consciousness feeling split; one part incredibly intrigued and focused on this sudden, deeper, calming breath, wondering why, and the other part still trying to decipher what Gerard was getting to. All of this happened over only a minute or two before, suddenly, Gerard, still at the front of the room, said *the* thing. A particular 'thing' that effectively dropped the shock right on me, and the jolt of that shock was a major ethical let down that was now my responsibility to say something about. It was now on me to have to strongly and openly disagree for the good of all of us involved. At this point in my working life, I was still figuring out confrontation. Never having been a fan, and still not entirely loving it now, I was still learning that all-important leadership skill of speaking up when it was needed. In this moment, the opportunity to practise that was thrust upon me, and it slowly dawned on me that my body had realised this and attempted to adequately prepare me in the meantime.

Because it was not an official research study, I can only go by what the experience felt like to me first-hand. It felt like my body had picked up on a tone, or just the general uncertain nature of what Gerard was – or wasn't – saying, and almost defaulted to what it knew. What it *knew* was the breathing and presence practice I had been cultivating consistently over the previous few years, strengthened by my recent foray into teaching it. It defaulted to what I had been practising around managing my stress and emotions, and in this moment that practice was exactly what I needed in order to be calm, clear, and coherent enough to openly disagree with and push back on what felt like an attack to me. My voice shook as I spoke, whether from the shock of the unexpected statement made, from the nerves that still existed for me, or perhaps from both. In any case, despite my shaky voice, I could say what I needed to.

I could articulate clearly that I disagreed, explain why it was now an ethical issue that concerned all of us, detail why so they understood, and stand my ground when they initially tried to deny the facts I had laid out. My mindfulness practice had come in with its seemingly golden cape and held the fort while I said a difficult thing, even though it felt hard and uncomfortable, and there was a big internal reaction happening for me that I had to communicate through. It grounded me enough and kept me present and mentally clear. In the end, my having the capacity to do that was a big step in how I developed and showed my leadership, even if I was not in the actual position of a 'leader' in this case. It was a formative experience that showed me it was possible and gave me a lived experience example of *how* exactly it was possible. It was also my last day working with them. I left clear I had done the right thing ethically.

Since then, I have had many an uncomfortable, challenging, voice-and-hand shaky conversation both as a leader and with other leaders. I still do not particularly enjoy them, but I have enjoyed the feeling and benefits of leaning on the tools of mindfulness each time, and I have only got better at navigating them. Not perfect, because we are all human and that is important to remember, but improved. Despite not enjoying these moments as much, I have also grown an appreciation of my capability in handling them. I have watched how I use these mindfulness tools to navigate the conversations so that I am also better able to demonstrate and lead the conversation with more emotional awareness – emotional intelligence – at the same time. Having the mindfulness to navigate the challenges leaves more room to ensure we do not lose the emotional intelligence along the way. Emotional intelligence that helps us as leaders to remember and behave as if there is more than one human experience happening in the conversation at the same time and to go forth and continue to navigate leadership challenges with that awareness. All of these skills in moving through uncomfortable moments and conversations have ultimately led me to making better, more effective leadership decisions.

Micro-Management Is No-No Management

Nothing inspires team members less than feeling like their managers or peers are constantly looking over their shoulder at the work they are doing. It is a lot like having to reverse parallel park your car in front of a crowd; it always feels harder to nail first go, and the pressure of the watching crowd of people often means you make mistakes you wouldn't normally. But then you practically perfect it next time you have to do it, and look around for the recognition but nobody is there to witness it. Except in a workplace context, you doing well regardless of whether anyone watched it happen in real time still benefits the business or the team in some way. You messing it up with everyone watching? This does not actually serve the overall goal, so nobody really wins and everybody is generally that bit unhappier or more uncomfortable.

In a workplace environment, it is important to remember what you are actually there for. Amongst a variety of things, we often view one main goal as helping each other and the business succeed in its stated goal and impact. So we must all continually look at and reassess behaviours that might impede us from achieving those goals, which includes exploring why we might carry out those behaviours in the first place. Micro-management often comes from a need to control, where there may be worry or fear that something might not get done in time, or adequately. However, sometimes, that need for control stems from an inability to relinquish that power. We often see it in managers and leaders who have not yet learned the art and practice of delegation. This art often includes understanding how delegation is actually quite beneficial for them and their contribution to the organisation, just as much as it is for the person carrying it out. This desire for perfectionism that we see carried out in management behaviour ends up acting as the antithesis of quality and, in some cases, speed and efficiency. This is where being mindful of 'why' you feel the need to linger over and question each part of a team member's process is so beneficial to understanding your behaviours, so that you can reflect on what would be more useful behaviours and habits working towards the overall goal; something you as a leader *are* in charge of. Then you can choose better.

The need for control in these matters lands more in the performative leadership space, where the optics on the outside might indicate you are 'doing' leadership, but the experience internally within the organisation tells a different story; one where you are not *being* a leader. Just a roadblock for progress. When you are constantly monitoring and attempting to control your team members in their work, it often has the opposite of the desired effect. Much like a child in a kitchen trying to help their parent make dinner, your intense and overbearing oversight slows things down in the process of the work being carried out, which, understandably, risks reducing quality output, as well as the volume of the output itself, quality or not.

So now, instead of being the leader and supporting your team to succeed in their roles, which directly impacts the progress towards the overall mission of the organisation, your actions have acted in sabotage, whether or not that was your intention. This decrease in quality work and productivity, sometimes even with the feeling of pressure at having failed so publicly in front of someone, has a direct impact on morale, decreasing motivation and drive. Often this is the pendulum pattern we will see in these manager-team member dynamics at this point; a manager, for whichever reason or motivation, steps too much into the over-management practice, which puts pressure on the team member and slows down their quality and output. This then has the manager feel like they need to step in even more in this way to control that output and improve it, which can worsen the conditions for the team members, exacerbating the poor results, leading to even poorer outcomes.

It is an unproductive cycle that the leader must then choose to stop, or risk contributing to the turnover, stress and burnout experienced within the team. Feeling the desire or need to take a tighter grip over tasks within your team can be a natural response to not seeing the results you would like. It can also be a natural response to the concern that the team member may not complete things soon or quickly enough. It seems like the logical response: to step in and make sure that those things *do* happen. This is where mindfulness becomes most pertinent for you to have as a continual practice.

Being mindful requires you to be attentive to how your actions or behaviours might make those around you feel. While you cannot be responsible for how someone responds emotionally or mentally, you can be responsible *for* how you show up in that engagement. And as a leader, that means being aware of how those you lead are responding to your overarching control in these scenarios. What you might see as 'helpful' and 'productive' might actually be met with the response in someone else as demotivating, frustrating, and even causing an increase in errors made. Your intention may be pure, and from the perspective of trying to help them and the whole team, but often this behaviour creates more problems than it solves in the long run. While some team members may thrive with this kind of oversight, and that may depend on things such as their level of experience, time in the role, or need for structure or accountability, it is important to understand your team members and what they need personally in order to thrive, rather than letting your own concerns drive such actions.

Often leaders will assume the pendulum swing in conversations about micro-management. They assume that if they 'can't step in and help' then they 'may as well step back and let people fail'; forgetting there is an entire middle section of behaviour and action in which you as a leader can exist in order to help support your team members. The first step, however, is recognising first and foremost whether there actually is an issue within the team or workflow to address, or whether it is an issue that requires self-reflection on the part of the leader. That self-reflection could help determine reasons as to *why* there is such a need for over-control here, even if it comes at the expense of the most well-functioning version of the team. This often becomes more of a delegation issue than a quality issue. Leaders, particularly if they have been promoted through these roles they are now managing, can often have a hard time letting go of some of the tasks involved in those roles that are now no longer theirs to carry out, but more to oversee. What happens, however, is they attempt to keep a version of control on these tasks while also contending with their new tasks in that leadership position, which – despite the convincing stories they may tell themselves – does not actually mean they are doing a great job just because they are doing more. These leaders are often setting themselves up for additional stress and a drop in quality by attempting to control it all.

If you see a team member of yours not performing to the right standard, or letting a task quality slip, instead of inviting yourself in to either try to control exactly how they do it, or constantly checking up on them to make sure they have done it, this is where you get to develop your leadership skills even more. It is an opportunity to bring that person into the conversation. Make sure they have the tools they need in order to understand and perform their role, including any support. Most importantly, you ensure they have these things by asking them directly what they might need to succeed, rather than assuming from your own perspective. As we have explored, and will continue to explore, as long as there are different people we are working with, there are different brains involved in those scenarios, all of which have different needs and ways they thrive or feel motivated. You can use your experience and understanding that you have developed over your life or career to help you create a foundation as a leader. Then a big part remaining of how you approach leadership can almost be from the perspective of not knowing, not assuming, but being willing to ask to find out.

Mindful leaders ask questions and are mindful of where their assumptions may be letting their leadership down.

This Is Not the Goal of Mindfulness, but a Happy Byproduct

One misconception when we talk about the practice of mindfulness in a workplace context can be that mindfulness should (only) be used for the sake of productivity, efficiency, or the bottom line. There is every reason to believe that these elements are benefited by these practices given the positive impact they have on how individuals function and manage their needs, and will be what most business owners and managers are understandably hoping for. Business is business after all, and will naturally have a requirement and desire to be profitable.

However, sometimes the focus of the financial bottom line can overshadow other just as valid motivations for integrating more mindfulness practices into leadership, and become *the* reason some leaders believe in the need for mindfulness. This misconceived version of what the practice is runs the risk of dismissing the other benefits from mindfulness practices that more naturally support a healthier, more successful workplace and culture; benefits such as a quality of experience, both in life and at work. By all means, use whatever motivation you need and is available to you or your people. We are not gatekeeping mindfulness and judging how people find it, or for what reasons they turn to the practices. At the same time, being aware of the risks of solely focusing on the external benefits and outcomes of mindfulness will help you to ensure you're creating a broader, more solid foundation in your practice that goes deeper than just 'how much money has been made as a result'.

When you make mindfulness only about productivity or a financial goal, for example, it remains superficial in nature. It risks becoming more mindfulness for show, a facade that has an ulterior motive than that of the wellbeing of yourself or your team members. When there is an ulterior motive, rather than a genuinely enjoyable side effect, it erodes trust and creates the expectation of a transactional experience. It opens up avenues for your team members to feel like there are conditions to their wellbeing and how they feel. If they can then not meet those conditions, there is the added stress of those things that otherwise support their wellbeing being taken away. Similarly with placing labels on yourself as an 'emotionally intelligent' leader or workplace, because you know that is the attractive thing to promote. When this happens, the risk is you, or members of your team, start to pretend there is more emotional intelligence without actually practising it as an ongoing skill. We have all come across those people who, when you meet them, it becomes intensely clear that they have read a certain book and are just following the steps suggested 'for success'. There lacks a depth in the interaction, even though they might be following the socially or professionally accepted 'steps', and you walk away with the sticky feeling of disingenuousness. This is why you can certainly enjoy the benefits that mindfulness and more emotionally intelligent leadership and workplaces bring, but the work is really in the actual practice of these things for the good of each human's experience. This is the number one 'why', that then allows all the other benefits to be experienced.

As leaders, it can be easy to focus only on the KPIs and targets, particularly around monetary goals. There is the ever-constant pressure – either placed on you by others or by yourself – to perform, to succeed, to achieve, so it is natural that these focuses tend to take the spotlight. For some, this can be one of the hardest aspects of bringing more of an emphasis on creating a more mindful and emotionally intelligent working environment. When we are told our goals and metrics of success are based so much on the numbers in this case, it can be a real challenge to peel our minds away from that being our sole focus, to introduce something else that does not seem related – at least on the surface. The words 'mindfulness' and 'emotional intelligence' hardly scream 'loads of money'. And yet, we know mindfulness training has a causal reduction in surface acting, emotional exhaustion, as well as increased job satisfaction (Hülsheger et al., 2013). Mindfulness also contributes to improved focus and persistence, enhanced information processing, more adeptness in evaluating goals and proactively working towards them, as well as reduced stress and burnout, all of which support better team connectedness, less staff turnover and absenteeism, as well as better communication skills (Awan et al., 2024) – all things that, again, directly serve your business goals.

You are also likely aware of a need to cultivate a team environment where interpersonal skills flourish. The reality of life is that life itself will still continue to go on outside of the workplace. This means that it is not enough to focus only on the stressors within the workplace environment, but to also acknowledge there will be stressors or events outside of the workplace that will at times inform how any one of your team members – including you – shows up. It is for the overall good of your culture and business to acknowledge this with mindfulness.

Even on a personal level for you as a leader, this becomes increasingly apparent. As a leader who genuinely practises mindfulness, which suggests you have more awareness of your stress levels and how you are then aware of how your team members are feeling, that creates a far more enjoyable and welcoming environment for your team to exist in. Even if the pressure is still there, perhaps you are in a more fast-paced industry, this ensures that burnout has the opportunity to stay at a minimum while motivation stays at a high. When leaders themselves are so stressed that everyone around them feels only, or mostly, tension, it creates issues in candour and transparency between your team members and you. Walking on eggshells is not a pleasant environment to exist in, and it also means that your people are far less likely to risk saying something that might crack one of those eggshells. You have the opportunity to build more trust with them in this way, so that you are getting more of the candid truth from your team members when it's needed, which helps you arm yourself with the information that you actually need in order to make the best possible decisions for everyone to progress forward.

Practice Does Not Equal Perfection, Especially in Relationships

Even without all the mindfulness and emotional intelligence, being in leadership is fraught with the expectation of perfection. This expectation works in two directions. First, the pressure you have from external parties. These are the parties who expect, or require, that you perform and succeed, sometimes seemingly at all costs. It could be higher-ups in the chain of command of the organisation, the board, and stakeholders of a company. It could even be pressure from your spouse at home, if the perception of 'success' is particularly important to them. These are the parties that expect perfectionism because they believe that to do less means less opportunity for the successes they are aiming for.

Secondly, there is the pressure that comes internally on, or against, yourself. It is this expectation that you can have on yourself that you do not make any mistakes. It is the stories your mind makes up about what it means if you are not perfect and do make a misstep, mistake, or wrong turn. It is the fear or worry of shame of what happens to your reputation in the eyes of others if you show that you are, in fact, human, which means you also fall foul of human error. It is the worry of losing the respect or attention of those whom you manage if you do not know every answer, or have to learn something by doing it the wrong way first.

Leadership is fraught with this kind of pressure, and it will come from every possible direction if we just set our minds to looking for it. Confirmation bias in the way our brains work almost ensures it. When we have decided something is true, our brain's confirmation bias sets out to find proof that it is true, because our brain's main inherent job is to keep us safe. It keeps us safe by continuing the status quo. Whether this proof is *probable* or just possible does not matter to the stories caught up in the information the confirmation bias seeks. What it thinks matters is simply what it has *decided*; that if you are not a perfect leader, if you make mistakes in your work or how you lead, that you have then sufficiently (and successfully) failed.

It is a self-told story only, of course, and yet these pressures still exist and continue to be perpetuated. Goals and KPIs are set for leaders and *by* leaders that expect results that are close to perfection and do not leave much room to allow for human error and learning opportunities. This is all despite a noted absence of perfectionism having a direct relationship with performance. In a study by Zhao and Huang (2025), perfectionism in leadership environments is explored, where they found and even referenced previous research in the field that shows there is no direct relationship between obsessive work passion – which could be seen as a nicer way of naming something that results from perfectionism – and performance outcomes. This research implies that striving for perfection is not actually as useful as we have all been led to believe culturally, since it does not correlate with better job performance and instead might actually lead to disengagement and burnout.

It begs the question when we do reintroduce mindfulness into the fray: When we now know that perfectionism does not actually lead to better performance outcomes, why do we continue to expect perfectionism in how we practise mindfulness? We encourage showing up more mindfully because we know it can create more supportive work environments and cultivate more emotional intelligence. Yet, when we err and have a moment where we are perhaps not as mindful as we could have been, we judge ourselves. When a leader's mind is particularly busy during a mindfulness practice one day, or several days, I have watched them immediately disparage themselves over it. This includes telling themselves how bad at mindfulness they are, how they have just wasted their time practising *all for nothing*, before getting up out of their seat entirely frustrated. Only to spend the rest of their day feeling like they have failed in this venture, possibly perpetuated by further behaviour that displays as particularly unmindful in itself.

These leaders are so preoccupied with their perceived failings that they are already missing the opportunity of the entire practice. That opportunity being that they can practise noticing what their experience is in each moment, which is really the point of the practice in any case. This then assists them to cultivate a similar kind of empathy for when one of their team members, for example, gets likewise frustrated at something that did not go as well as they hoped. This empathy leads to the leader's opportunity to effectively counsel or mentor them through that. When we are able to understand how something feels, regardless of the cause of that feeling, we are better able to at the very least show compassion and empathy to others who are feeling that, with the possibility of even more so being able to help them navigate better through it. It starts with being able to notice it and acknowledge it.

When people, such as your team members, feel a pressure to be more mindful without the adequate understanding, support, or demonstration of the tools that show what that even means in the context of the workplace and that particular cultural environment, it can feel like additional pressure at first. Similarly for leaders who respond to it as just another task on their list. This pressure can be exacerbated in cultures of perfectionism. We can cultivate cultures of perfectionism even in instances where they are not done so via explicit instructions given. Cultures of perfectionism can also come from the pressure leaders put on themselves, which then extends outwardly to their team as a byproduct. When leaders hold perfectionistic standards for themselves, they may – intentionally or unintentionally – enforce a perfectionistic standard on their team members. This transfer of a perfectionistic demand from leaders onto their employees can lead to increased stress and anxiety amongst team members. While some people will insist they work well under this kind of pressure, this high performance pressure in workplaces where such a demand is out of context for the role can harm the workplace culture and the wellbeing of the team members involved by triggering negative emotional responses.

These kinds of outcomes are possible regardless of whether this is deliberately extended out as expectations placed upon their team explicitly, or unconsciously via a leader who puts extensive amounts of pressure on themselves to be perfect. Perfectionism through direct yet unachievable goals and measures, or even unfair punishment in response to mistakes made, can be just as damaging as leaders outwardly stressing the importance of their own perfect behaviour. This internal pressure and standard from leaders sends the message of the goal of perfection, while at the same time creating confusion amongst team members who might feel that pressure without it actually being a directive. Yet, instead of it being a motivation, as some leaders perceive it to be, this kind of performance pressure can lead to the kind of emotional strain on teams that hinders their own job performance, increases issues in interpersonal communication, and leads to feelings of inadequacy or burnout. We might become far less likely to take chances, even in communicating with our fellow team members, if we are worried about saying or doing the wrong thing. Fewer chances taken lead to fewer opportunities to learn differently or strengthen skills we might actually do well without having the positive feedback helping us to reinforce those behaviours.

High expectations for 'perfect' levels of job performance risk increasing experiences of excessive resource depletion. While some leaders may see that as 'taking the initiative' and 'using all resources available' to get the job done at hand, it can be harmful when this kind of cognitive overload and depletion adversely impacts employee motivation and performance; even in leaders themselves. If we continually strive to meet unrealistic standards, as a leader or as pressure put on our teams, motivation quickly diminishes and self-criticism sharply increases. When we might be afraid to bring something up during a check-in or in a meeting as an issue, simply because it is not to a perfect standard, leaders are missing out on the opportunity to help their team learn, grow, and develop confidence. Despite this method being typically considered a healthy way of communicating at work in order to continue progressing things well, it can risk being bypassed for fear that the team member might then demonstrate they are not, in fact, perfect.

Without creating secure spaces for this kind of intra-team communication, you as a leader might be unconsciously suggesting to everyone involved they should be criticised for not having it done perfectly, regardless of whether this criticism remains internal or has the opportunity to be given by anyone externally. Enough criticism without opportunities to make mistakes in order to learn and grow quickly festers into an unmotivated and unsatisfied team. This is a much more challenging issue to overcome in a workplace after the fact, though not necessarily impossible.

When you have a stressed-out, unmotivated, critical, fearful workforce, it makes it really challenging to have a healthy leadership relationship with your team members. They may feel more closed off, responding with half of the information you might actually need unless prompted, even avoiding you or other leadership in extreme cases. In many cases, that can also be their experience of you in return, whether you intend it to be or not. While the goal of workplace relationships is not necessarily to become the closest of friends who share everything – this is entirely possible in some cases but, naturally, professionally, never the expectation or goal – having a healthy rapport in your workplace relationships will help you to have the information you need in order to perform your role to the best of your abilities. This includes helping to develop a healthier, more satisfying, and even happier workplace culture for all to enjoy. You, as a leader, cannot be responsible for everything that every single team member may be feeling, but as a leader, you have the opportunity to help create a more welcoming environment for each person to thrive.

This is why it is important to be mindful of your subconscious behaviour and thoughts, and how they are presenting outwardly. When you are mindful of when you are feeling stress, for example, you are then able to put measures into place to mitigate the outward effects on others this stress might have, without dismissing it for yourself – because dismissing it further buries your awareness, but not the manifestation of it in your or others' experiences. How do you learn how to be self-aware? The more mindfulness you practise consistently, the more you become attuned to your body, your mind, and your experience in each moment. Many people often want what is really the productivity hacks; things like how to time block their day to focus and how to schedule out their week. They desire these solutions without recognising that it is understanding the fundamentals that is most important to how we then experience these mindful solutions in the workplace. These tips are helpful, but they lack effectiveness in the face of not having the self-awareness to even understand something is going on for you in the first place that might be causing or contributing to their challenge in focus or why they are over-scheduling themselves.

Even a seemingly simple breathing practice can give you information. This can be in a variety of experiences, such as depending on how challenging it might feel to take adequate inhales or lengthen any exhales, or even if trying to breathe a bit deeper or exhale a bit longer brings up any unexpected emotions. For example, finding a deeper breathing practice challenging – unexpectedly, rather than related to exercise or other health issues – might, for example, suggest that you could be holding physical tension that is limiting your ability to breathe deeper or exhale longer. From there, you can then know where to start to explore further. This is not an opportunity for self-diagnosis, nor can this book provide one, but it is an opportunity to become aware in the first place that, in this case, there might even be tension in your physical experience. Similarly to meditation practices, where persistent thoughts show up despite your best attempts to find 'a quiet mind' – a common yet misguided goal for those who meditate. The opportunity here being that noticing your thoughts when you give yourself and your mind space to notice them can give you information about what, simply, might be on your mind, or what thoughts are taking up your mental energy or focus. While the experience of a more zen-like experience during meditation can feel nice, the benefit of the practice lies in getting to know what is present for yourself in this moment. Put into applicable practice, when you as a leader actually notice the persistent thoughts that are otherwise usually running around subconsciously as you go about your day, you might be able to better understand where your worries or concerns are, why you might be reacting to someone's tone in a particular way, or why you might be feeling a bit stressed so that you can then either address it, or at least communicate better around it.

Building Your Mindful Leadership Practice

Creating a Sustainable Mindfulness Routine

One mistake I see time and time again is that, upon learning about mindfulness or having opportunities to dive in the most significantly they may have ever been able to thus far, some participants in mindfulness will immediately attempt to adopt the 'all or nothing' approach. This approach has them going from virtually zero practice or priming beforehand directly into attempting to implement three hours of a daily meditation practice that has them up well before the Australian summer sunrise, in addition to all the other 'biohacking' methods heavily filling their day just to fit it all in, before collapsing exhausted into bed each night.

It is well-documented that different bodies and brains respond differently to the variety of wellbeing interventions available; therefore, the challenge is fraught with attempts to apply mindfulness practices expecting exacting results. Biologically, different sexes or ages often require different amounts of sleep, prefer exercising at different times of the day, and thrive differently with different forms of movement. Neurologically and psychologically, each person's brain responds to different stimuli, or lack of it, in different ways; trauma can inform the effectiveness of different practices, including even where certain practices might exacerbate symptoms or stress. Hormones can determine efficacy, and external environments or events can impact internal responsiveness to different practices on different days.

It is also important to keep context in mind when setting out to improve your wellbeing through mindfulness practices, whether you intend to apply them to your leadership or not. Each person's day is made up of 24 hours, but each person's 24 hours involve vastly different requirements and demands. The phrase 'everyone has the same 24 hours in the day' sets a damaging standard to expectations and needs because each person's 24 hours is impacted uniquely. Holding the expectation that they optimise every – often extended – waking moment, lest they be considered lazy, is one of the most dangerous 'wellbeing' rhetorics out there. While enthusiasm towards your brand new or newly reinvigorated mindfulness practice is sure to assist you in getting started and continuing your practice as you develop the routine and habit, it can also lead to an over-ambitious approach that is ultimately detrimental to why you wanted to begin in the first place.

In one of the most common questions I receive when I facilitate for groups, the topic of '*when, for how long, and how often, should I meditate?*' will inevitably arise. Given that the experience of mindfulness interventions is largely subjective, even in controlled research studies, often the answer is very simply this:

Practice your mindfulness whenever you are able to do it most consistently, in a way that is as achievable as possible.

So while the desire and motivation – and influencer advice – may have you wanting to dive right into those three-hour, 4am meditation sessions, this approach may not be sustainable for you over a longer period of time in context to your lifestyle. It may also not even bring in the desired or intended results; a longer meditation or mindfulness session does not automatically equal better results because of the longer time spent. It may have you missing out on valuable and necessary sleep at night, or it could risk you missing out on the connection of community – whether with your family, or your more external community – if you are not as available because of your practice requirements. In anything, what you say 'yes' to means you are saying 'no' to something else, and when it comes to mindfulness there are likely things that are not such a loss. But allowing your mindfulness practice to become too all-consuming, where you are then saying 'no' to virtually everything else in an attempt to practise puritanically, it further exacerbates the imbalance you might have initially experienced, just at the opposite end of the pendulum. Not only that, but the law of diminishing returns is likely to come into effect that then has you seeing your results plateau beyond a certain amount of practice each day. Besides that, a mindfulness practice while you isolate from applying it in your real life speaks more to individualism in wellbeing, where much of the benefit comes from the collectivism approach; that being how we work on our own wellbeing, in community with and for each other, we yield far greater results both individually and collectively within the systems we exist in – those same systems that have the power to contribute to our thriving or lacking wellbeing. And as a leader? You want to ensure you prioritise accordingly towards collectivism.

So if three-hour meditation sessions do not appeal to you or sound reasonable for your lifestyle, you are not failing. It also does not mean that you are not dedicated enough to your mindfulness practice. There are just more effective ways you can benefit from it. Generically, broad advice for applying mindfulness looks at what you can do that is very simple. This will depend on what kind of mindfulness practice you are applying in practice, but for applying breath work practices or meditation, a few minutes at a time, consistently, is found to be far more effective than holding off until you can spend that half hour – very inconsistently in any case – every two or so weeks. Five slow, deliberate breaths while being present to those inhales and exhales every day are far more likely to provide mindful benefits than an hour *maybe* every three or four weeks. Emphasising this consistency over the duration of time you are spending on it at each time will help you to build a more sustainable habit. It is important to remember that mindfulness is very much about a lifestyle approach that can serve you for the rest of your actual life; it is not the 'get rich quick' scheme of leadership.

When you are practising your mindfulness more consistently, it also becomes much easier to grasp even beyond the habit. While extended periods of mindfulness can be really enjoyable, like a morning at the beach, a few hours in nature, or an afternoon of gentle yoga for example, when you are practising more consistently – such as most days in some way, even if in small ways – it is much easier for you to implement mindfulness into more of your everyday interactions. This is what turns a mindfulness practice into actually *being* mindful.

A leader who spends one Sunday a month in some kind of mindful retreat tends to be practising mindfulness far more for themselves than the leader who is actively practising some form of mindfulness each and every day. Taking time out in environments that help you to unwind stress is important, but it becomes far more applicable when the practice is more frequent; even if those more frequent practices are shorter.

Consider this: You might have a real problem with stress, in the sense that you struggle to truly unwind. Perhaps your nervous system does not make you feel like it is safe to, in case things 'fall apart' if you pause to breathe for too long, telling you the story that you must hold a tight grip in order to hold it all together. This could mean that any unwinding activity in a large dose could feel like a lot for your system to handle; maybe even too much. In this case, waiting for your monthly relaxation massage can only do so much for this. What might be more effective in helping your system to even get on board with the relaxation strategies in the first place is smaller, shorter approaches to mindfulness practices, more often. Things like sitting down for five minutes at the beginning or end of each day, or taking five minutes' worth of diaphragmatic breaths while you count them on your fingers. In this scenario, your physical body and even your active mind might have more of an opportunity to get used to those breaths. Often when we begin breathwork practices, for example, our 'lengthened' breath is still quite short and shallow. But the more you practice it consistently, the more your body gets used to the deeper, longer breaths, so the sooner you are able to enjoy even deeper, fuller breaths. This simpler, more consistent approach helps you work on the tools in each moment now that support you, which then go on to support your team members around you. Where the 'once a month' approach might feel good – in which case, continue enjoying it – but does not as effectively equip you with the same tools. Similar to how we do not expect children to go straight from entering first grade to operating at a 12th grade level; it is not just about building the habit strength, but about actually teaching your whole physiological system *how* to put it into practice.

Another really useful way to develop a sustainable mindfulness routine is to make it feel like less of 'just another thing' you have to do, and more like something you enjoy doing that is *easy*. There is a lot to be said for simplicity, and this is not the first time you would have heard to keep it simple; cliche exists for a reason, and that reason is because it is most often true. Habit-stacking is the strategy of building new habits by attaching them to existing ones. Similar to why you might put things away in the same spot each time so you always know where to find them, when you link your new mindfulness practices to existing daily routines, or make simple 'rules' for how and when you do them, it becomes a lot easier for your mind to do them. One simple habit I implemented some years back was utilising my smart watch – which can also be done with any smart phone and the apps available. I made it a habit that when I turned out the light each night for bed and got myself comfortable, before I would roll over and try to go to sleep, I would use the appropriate app to do just one minute of deep, diaphragmatic breathing. The app was set to one minute where it would vibrate for the length of the inhale, giving you time to allow for the exhale before it would start again, including a visual cue if that's your preference. This helped me to spend just this moment settling in, setting it up as a habit and a signal for my brain that it was time to sleep, and from my own experience, I found it helped to focus my mind from any of the errant thoughts that were running around, towards sleep. It also made me feel more settled. What made it work was the habit-stacking and routine of it. I already, naturally, had the routine of turning out the light on my bedside table when I was ready for sleep. This new ritual was also simple to implement because it was not an extended length of time that made it feel like just another to-do on my list; it was a single, actual minute. The simplicity made it achievable, which meant I was practising into more consistently every day.

Another even simpler approach could be for the two or so minutes you are brushing your teeth, if your sinuses allow, you can also stack that time of brushing to include deep diaphragmatic breaths in and out through your nose. This doesn't add anything to your calendar or to-do list, and there is no extra time necessary to find, but for at least once – maybe two or more times – a day, you've suddenly built this breathing habit because you haven't made it complicated to do.

Simple Exercises for Developing Mindfulness

Developing your own mindfulness practice is not a copy-and-paste approach, nor will it be that way for your team. Often, when beginning to engage with mindfulness, many leaders initially want to be told exactly what will work, seeking mostly the ready-made tactics they can put into place without any further thought or inner enquiry; time-blocking tools here, meeting management there. They are also looking for templated approaches for their team or organisation, often skipping the very important middle – self-awareness. While having someone guide you through a process, much like how a yoga teacher or personal trainer does, is so useful, the real practice is in practising self-awareness; and then leading by example for your team to witness.

Experimenting with what different practices work for you at different times of the day, or during different moods, is important for you to understand how you respond. Each practice will also present differently for different physical and mental abilities as well, so it is important to adjust – or support and enable others to adjust – as needed. Then remembering that the practice itself is the goal, and not so much the response itself, once you have reached that point. There are some simple practices that can act as your starting point to explore, some of which we have already covered.

- Diaphragmatic breathing – this is the practice of breathing in deeper towards the bottom of the lungs, so that they press down on the diaphragm muscle. It is often referred to as belly breathing, because the visual result is that the stomach is moved forward out of the way, caused by the lungs and diaphragm moving further down. This has been found to help to reduce perceived feelings of stress, which is said to then further help you to think a bit clearer. This is particularly so when the breath is equal – where the inhale and the exhale match each other in length, or when the exhale is slightly longer than the inhale. Box breathing, or square breathing, has also been found to be beneficial for participants' wellbeing, so long as holding the breath is safe for the participant to practice. This is where the deeper diaphragmatic breath is practiced, but there is a pause – a holding of the breath – at the top of the inhale, as well as at the bottom of the exhale, so if you were to draw the depiction of the breath, it might look like a square, or a rectangle depending on how long you are holding your breath for in relation to the actual breath. It is important to note that there are some health and physical conditions where holding the breath is not recommended, including but not limited to conditions such as pregnancy, anxiety, or high blood pressure. Please ensure you are aware of your own limitations from your medical professional first – and remember this also might be a reality for your team members as well, whether you are privy to that information or not.
- Forest bathing – research has shown that forest environments can help to lower cortisol levels, heart rate, and blood pressure, in comparison to urban areas. It indicated that forest 'bathing' – spending time in the forest without agenda – can potentially develop as a preventative health strategy, when it comes to helping to mitigate some of the health impacts from stress due to the calming effect on the body that natural settings can have, thanks to an increase in parasympathetic nerve activity (Park et al., 2010). This will naturally be determined by which area in the world you live in, the weather

and climate, your accessibility needs, or what exposures might be more dangerous for you uniquely, including allergies.

- Body scan rotation – practicing presence through the body scan rotation activity can help you to be in the active practice of noticing what is showing up, without needing to respond to it. The body scan, or body rotation, practice involves resting in a comfortable position and taking your awareness on a rotation around your body as it 'scans' for awareness. You might start at your fingers on your right hand, moving up the arm and then down the right side of the body, before going to do the same on the left side, for example. By isolating your awareness on each part of your body at a time, you practice noticing sensation – or even a lack of sensation – without needing to do anything to change your current state. Body scans have been found to be beneficial in lowering the heart rate and reducing blood pressure, as well as reducing the experience of perceived stress (Bartlett et al., 2019), assisting participants in their emotional regulation, supportive for chronic pain management, and increasing self-awareness.
- Journalling – whether this is journalling your literal to-do list each morning so that you can be more mindful of how you spend your energy and attention each day, or a practice of appreciation journalling where you take note of things that you appreciate each day, journalling can be a useful way to practice mindfulness by bringing your attention to the present moment. The very functional version of journalling out your to-do list – which may be less focused on whole sentences than traditional journalling, and more focused on the note-taking style – is a mindful way to direct your attention to what you would like, or need it, to be focused on. A to-do list is a version of practicing presence, making it a lot easier for your mind to focus on what is right in front of you, rather than an open attention span that has not been given any direction. Appreciation journalling is also a mindful way of directing your attention to things you would like to acknowledge, but is more open to the theme you choose to focus on. Appreciation journalling can have a theme around your work – what you appreciate about your job, how you showed up on that day, your clients you got to work with, even the money you got to make, or it could be more personal – where it helps you to focus on things that you appreciate in your life outside of work, whether it be your relationships, your home, your pets, or your health. It is a practice in presence helping you to take notice of your current circumstances, further working with the reticular activating system in your brain – the confirmation bias that you are directing to notice more of any particular thing. In practicing this and directing it to notice things to appreciate, your brain is primed to more easily notice more, similar things to appreciate in your day to day.
- Using environmental or digital cues – sometimes mindfulness is not about an activity, but a routine or environmental factor. Your mindfulness practice can be more about how you set about working, with time-blocking for example. Time-blocking is where you set a timer for a certain amount

of time – be it 20 minutes or an hour – and focus on a task for that length of time. Then when the timer goes off, you give yourself a small break, which could be your tea break, a social break, a stepping-outside break – whatever helps you shift your position to refresh before you come back to it and do it again, with either the same task or a different one. There are two factors involved here that are just as important as the other; the block of time is important as your prompt to focus only on your set goal or task. The timer allows you to put your other devices or distractions away, reassuring your mind that you will get to enjoy that distraction when the timer goes off. The practice in mindfulness is the presence you put to the thing in front of you. The other important factor is the break in between. Whether that break is five or 30 minutes – and perhaps you set a timer for this too, if you find you get distracted easily – it is important to allow between tasks and mindful moments. Other cues could be using different music or sounds, scents, or even computer windows for different types of activities. For example, you might have a playlist that is for deep focus and comprises lyric-less music that suits your needs, and a different playlist for preparing for a meeting or presentation. Similarly, different windows can operate for differing tasks; if you study and also have work to do, you might have one window or browser that you conduct all of your study or research on, and use a separate window or browser for work-related activities – either option allowing you to have as many tabs open as you desire within each respective window. This can help you remain mindful and present on what you must focus on in that moment, helping to at least reduce distractions from outside of your current focus zone.

Tools for Mindful Communication and Meetings

Another example of how you could apply this in your own leadership practice is before or after meetings. Whether the meetings are in person or online, before you step into the room, make it a habit to take five slow breaths. Then again, when each meeting ends, you could take another five slow breaths back at your desk to transition between one thing and whatever comes next. Once you get more comfortable with things like this, it can also be beneficial to the extended team to introduce it as a (new) normal way that you start meetings. When I was working more internally leading a team, I introduced and led the new habit of taking a quick moment for each person to acknowledge their 'honourable mentions'. This usually worked during the weekly team meetings, where it was an honourable mention for the previous week; something they could name that they are appreciating. I specifically used the word 'appreciate' rather than 'gratitude' in order to avoid too-commonly used buzzwords – and in some cases, to avoid the eye rolls – but we implemented it with an explanation of why.

Our brain operates on a confirmation bias, which means that it will always be looking for proof of whatever we are believing or assuming. It is the brain's way of keeping you safe by maintaining the perceived status quo, where it will interpret information in a way to confirm its own (your own) assumptions. In this case, I had noticed that my team were hyper-focusing more and more on negativity in their day-to-day. Not only were they not feeling good as a result of this negative bias – something which our minds tend towards naturally in the first place (Baumeister et al., 2001) – but they were also missing out on noticing opportunities where they could improve their different situations. By only focusing on all the negative, and then making that negative focus even louder by fixating on it in conversations and update meetings, their minds were not paying attention to the growth opportunities or ways forward; just the negative issue at hand. I introduced this new habit at the beginning of our weekly team meetings by being open and honest about why, without blame. I shared with them what I had noticed, that I had a desire to help and support them more in this, and why I had chosen this particular mindfulness practice. I also acknowledged that it might feel a bit awkward at first. Even when there are explicitly no expectations of anybody sharing anything personal, beginning mindfulness practices within a workplace team can sometimes feel a bit vulnerable and have a sense of awkwardness; at least when you first start off. As a leader, it is important to both explain the reasoning behind why, and to also be willing to lead and go first. For a few weeks when beginning those meetings, I made a point of reminding them of the *why* behind why we were now doing this. When we are caught up in the uncomfortable moment, it can be easy to forget why we are doing it in the first place. As a leader, you get to be that reminder. In those first few weeks, I also made a point of going first to give them an example. Having an example of what this practice could be or look like helps to spark ideas, and it also helps to reduce awkwardness when someone else has said something first. Eventually, I began to put the offer out and ask if anyone else wanted to go first, and from there it became a habit that even the loudest of protesters – who were mostly protesting in jest – would defend it.

This simple practice might seem tokenistic, but when you are pro-actively supporting your team to start to be mindful of how they are thinking and speaking – without making them wrong otherwise – you are leading and supporting them to grow. This is your job. It is also important to remember that oftentimes, the simplest practices that are good for us can also be the most difficult for us to remember to do. In workplaces, there is often a perception – sometimes imagined, and sometimes very real – that ideas do not matter unless they are new, fresh, innovative, and big. So it is natural for anyone, leader or not, to feel like a simple solution, even if valid and backed by research, is not going to be seen as clever enough. This is your opportunity as a leader to put your ego-check to good use by reminding those you lead that while there can certainly be value in the big ideas, sometimes less is more and coming back to the simple basics will yield more long-term results.

If the previously mentioned forest bathing is not quite accessible in your work time, as it likely will not be for many, the practice of implementing walking (or 'moving') meetings where possible could be your next best option to help you and your team members to get out and into the fresh air. For the sake of inclusivity, 'walking' may not be an accessible option for all, so it's important to ensure that this option suits all inclusive needs and is accessible for all in whichever way you deliver it.

Whether you are near to nature – some grass or a few trees – or in an urban city environment, this can double up on something else that is on your schedule without necessarily adding to the sense of overwhelm that can often come with trying to fit 'just one more thing' in. For in-person meetings, if you can determine if your meeting can work well as a walking meeting, or even a walk to the coffee shop option, you give the opportunity for more mindfulness and ease for all parties involved. Often there is more comfort with open dialogue when people are walking together, rather than facing each other in a closed-in room. It is often easier for people to share more naturally side by side with someone without being faced with the confrontation or vulnerability – whether intended or not – of that face-on interaction. Again, different needs for accessibility will determine whether this is an effective approach. While some neurodivergent conditions may thrive with this approach, it may not suit someone who has a hearing impairment and may rely on visual cues, such as reading sign language or lip reading. This checking in and awareness becomes part of your mindfulness practice.

For those who have use of their body in this way, walking meetings also encourage better blood flow and lymphatic drainage, even for gentle walks not intended for explicit exercise purposes. Not only can this have the added benefit of helping to improve the energy and wellbeing of each person, helping them to feel more well in general, the change in the environment and respiratory rate, or even moving from an air-conditioned environment to fresher air, can assist cognitively as well. For meetings between remote teams held online, it can be useful to encourage or normalise participants taking these meetings while on a walk, or even on their at-home treadmill or walking pad, should they choose. As leaders, it is important to give clear permission for your team members to choose ways to show up that support their attentional energy, focus, and wellbeing as well. A walk during a 9am meeting, for example, might suit them much better than being forced to walk in the midday heat during their lunch break, or trying to fit it in before or after work where they may have other commitments, or it may be too dark at that point in the day for them to feel comfortable enough in their safety.

Preparation Isn't Meant to Equal Perfection, and That's the Point

Communication itself, even when done with more intention, can remain a tricky practice. It is so influenced by a variety of factors that can be known, as well as factors that will always remain unknown, that it can feel impossible for anyone to adequately prepare for. One misunderstanding about communicating mindfully comes about from people's hope they can do a good job, and that is misunderstanding the level of control you will have in how a conversation will go. There is only so much you can truly prepare ahead of conversations you anticipate being difficult or challenging, and the risk in preparing mindfully lies in believing that the preparation will be enough for the conversation to go exactly 'as planned'. The mindfulness is only in part in the preparation ahead of time. Much of the mindfulness practice in communicating with others, particularly as a leader, lies in being present to how the conversation is actually going in the moment; whether it is how you anticipated it to go or not. Too often we see leaders, particularly on the public stage, go into certain conversations with their talking points and not being present to what they are actually being asked, or how their pre-planned responses are being responded to in the actual conversation. No matter how much you prepare, the real-time conversation might go vastly differently to your simulated examples you went through prior, and being a mindful leader requires the element of both preparation and presence.

Presence gives leaders the ability to build trust, even through moments where they can acknowledge they do not know the answer to something rather than continuing to repeat pre-loaded responses that do not quite fit. This kind of presence can also at times be pleasantly surprising for those involved. Many people experience stress in the anticipation of important conversations, even when those are potentially beneficial conversations for them or others involved. This can show up from things like job interviews, to salary increase requests, to expressing concern or discontent with the behaviour of the other party. Yet, when you are able to practise presence in yourself and to the other person, it also allows you to experience how the conversation is really going. In some cases, it can actually go much better than the worry or stress indicated otherwise. Sometimes the job interview feels really natural and results in a positive outcome, or the salary conversation is met with an easy agreement and plan, or the other person is able to hear your concerns, acknowledge them, and discuss a reparation plan moving forward.

There is no direct statistic able to be given around the correlation between mindfully preparing for certain kinds of communication and the guaranteed positive outcome, but being mindful about how we communicate can improve how we respond to moments in real time. It can also help to ensure the other person feels validated or understood, regardless of how much you do or do not agree with them about the issue at hand.

3 Self-Awareness as a Skill

Self-awareness is much like the 'what are we doing?' aspect of mindfulness and presence. Where mindfulness and practices in presence are the foundation or basis of where you could begin, self-awareness could be seen as the *act* of the practice. This is where you enquire: What am I exploring as part of these practices?

Our brains will look for efficiency and where it can approach an activity or task in a rote method. Self-awareness, while not necessarily always 'hard' or 'work', still requires that focused attention. It's not simply a matter of listing off your times tables because you, at one point, learned the rhythm through repetition enough times. It requires active focus and intention as part of that practice.

Understanding the Role of Self-Awareness in Leadership

I was a 'checkout chick' at a local supermarket during my high school years, showing up weeknights, every Saturday and most Sundays with a happy face ready to win the *Best Cashier Ever* award I was up against in my own head. Once I settled into the groove of what would end up being three years spent there right up until high school graduation, I began to notice something about customers coming through my checkout. Many were genuinely lovely, or at least pleasant enough. It was some of the others, however, that really caught my attention. These were the type that clearly were not enjoying their time grocery shopping, and as far as that went, I can't really blame them. I always tended to figure they had something else going on in their day, or that they, like me, did not love grocery shopping and also didn't possess much of a poker face to hide it. Regardless of why, once I had noticed, I made it almost a mission to ensure I did not let it change how I treated them. I didn't lay on the 'happy' too thick either, but instead chose to stay grounded and steady in it. I chose to be present, open, and avoid assuming negative intent. I didn't know these words to use for this decision at the time, but in retrospect it has become easier to recognise – like many things.

As per usual when a new customer started putting their groceries on the conveyor belt, I would smile and ask them how they were. A pretty standard

DOI: 10.4324/9781003632771-4

greeting, nothing complicated or fancy about it. If they did choose to respond beyond a grunt, sometimes the reply I got was something about how I was 'just being paid' to ask them that. Not realising then at the time how literally my autistic brain takes most things, that would confuse me, and my response probably indicated as such. It was somewhere in the area of 'Well… no. I just like to ask'. I'm still unsure what any 15-year-old is meant to say to that. In any case, I recall making a conscious decision to carry on as pleasantly as I was able to, whether that's the stubborn teenager who refused to let anyone else have a say over my mood or something else.

What would happen then was usually either one of two things: My continuing and genuine attempts at pleasantness to their abruptness, or in some cases rudeness, were enough to help bring them out of it. That's not to say a pleasant demeanour solved all of their problems. It either helped or helped them realise their tone, and that tone would noticeably shift. It was much like holding up a mirror to someone's behaviour or tone, but a mirror of opposites, where the contrast became too noticeable to ignore. Watching this play out from my vantage point behind the register looked as if they shook their head after a knock and snapped out of it. That was always a much more enjoyable outcome. The other outcome I noticed happen instead was, upon realising their mood or tone could not impact my level of pleasantness, the customer seemed to almost get grumpier. This is naturally all from my own subjective perspective and can't then be determined as factual accuracy. It is impossible to say for sure what was going on, but to my teenage brain, my good mood made them crankier because *they couldn't affect it.*

On the other hand, there is every chance their responses to me were entirely about me at all, ever in any of the cases, and this is how I perceived what happened purely based on my uneducated observation. I didn't possess the wherewithal to ask; nor would it have been appropriate in the context anyway. What I did know was that my experience was the decision to not let somebody else's mood be *my* mood, at any point, to the best of my ability. It is a fairly elementary example that has only been revealed in retrospect, and feels very much like an old nursery rhyme about sticks and stones, but there is an interesting takeaway to observe. This anecdotal correlation was imprinted in my internal gauge of behaviour from having and noticing these experiences.

The Inner Landscape of Leadership

Emotional intelligence requires the practice of self-awareness in order to flourish. I was no expert in this, particularly as a teen, but even then I innately knew enough about self-preservation to unknowingly be practising it in these moments. In a study of 22 leaders in successful Hungarian companies (Krén & Séllei, 2020) that aimed to understand how emotional intelligence influences organisational performance, one of the key competencies highlighted was self-awareness. From this study, it found that leaders who possessed high levels of self-awareness are better positioned to recognise and understand their own emotions. This in turn assists them to make better decisions and engage more effectively with their teams.

Put into context with my first job experience, I was able to know my own mood and emotions enough in those moments, and recognise the difference between those that were mine and those that were someone's whom I was serving. From an experience perspective, this meant that my practice of this kind of discernment ensured that not only my experience at work was not as impacted by external negativity, but that my performance in my role and rapport with customers was at a level the company was satisfied with. So again, while we can look at our earlier working experiences during high school or university and not take them as seriously because maybe 'they matter less' or we don't deem them as important to the work we may be doing now, there are still going to be valuable lessons there for you to reflect on if you go looking for them. That in itself is a practice of self-awareness that extends beyond just the present moment and notices what has come before leading up to the version of leader you are now, in this moment.

Moving forward then, leading others must start with how we lead ourselves. That doesn't mean that it is impossible to lead others without leading ourselves first, but rather speaks more to how we are always leading others through example; so if we are not aware of how we are leading ourselves, no amount of genuine attempts to lead others well will be as effective in the ways we are striving for, if our own behaviour or example is speaking for us in opposition otherwise. This is very similar to the 'do as I say, not as I do' mistake that is often made in all leadership contexts. Many parents will likely attest to this, noting that they have learnt that how they speak to their children becomes how their children speak to them; the behaviour that is normalised makes their children believe that is how best to behave.

With leadership, it is important to remember that it must start from somewhere, and it must be congruent with the message you are trying to imprint on the culture. A teacher teaching their students not to litter cannot go and then openly litter without, first, creating confusion with students in the process, and secondly, then subconsciously saying that this behaviour is in fact okay, which then leads to the risk of others – in this case the students – following suit; because what you do gives them the permission to also do.

Before you get to self-awareness being just another attempt at influencing behaviour however, first consider that this practice also allows you to recognise more easily what it is that *you* need. As a leader, and as a human, that in itself gets to be enough of a reason to develop these skills. Burnout is an ever-increasing experience, with stress disproportionately contributing to the rise in ill health, both physical and mental. At some point, it is time to start considering your quality of life while you are at work, just as much as in your personal time, instead of 'working to live', or in some instances, ***living to work.***

Taking care of your own physical and mental needs doesn't need to mean you are taking away from others around you in order to do so. It can actually be good for the people around you, if you do so mindfully. It's one thing to ignore your responsibilities in an effort to make it to the gym five days a week or an attempt to reach so-called enlightenment via a three-hour daily meditation. At some point, the people around you are going to need a little bit of your energy directed to what you are building together; whether that is your partner with contributions around the house or the kids, or your colleagues who are still waiting for that decision to be made or vital updates on information so they can go ahead and do their jobs. It's all in balance, and there is no one way to prescribe how much is considered 'too much' in this format. It's up to you to discern and to take that into consideration.

One thing we can be more certain of is this: Effective leadership begins within because how you lead is shaped by how well you understand yourself. If you understand, for example, that your emotions are running a bit higher than usual because of other events occurring in your life, without being self-aware of that, those big emotions risk coming out in the way you speak with your colleagues or team members, or how much more erratically you might be making decisions without due thought and consideration first. This may seem simple, and like something that's easy enough to default to by just dealing with the outcomes of it all, but it plays a big role in how it contributes to how people feel around you and the culture of the team you are leading. One day of a bad mood can be easy for others to put aside. But the ongoing experience of daily bad moods and unreasonable decisions over the course of weeks, even months, will alienate the people around you; especially if they're confused about what's going on. People, much like the younger versions of ourselves as children, tend to see behaviour as it is and focus mostly on their own experience of that behaviour. Children will tend to assume blame onto themselves if their parents are in a bad mood and lash out with a sharper tongue than usual. As adults, while we have much more developed brains and abilities to better emotionally regulate, all we know out of context is our own experience of something; not the understanding, and consequential compassion, of what might be driving it if we are spoken to in a certain way. This doesn't mean you need to share personal details you aren't comfortable sharing, or that might be inappropriate to share in a workplace. But self-awareness also isn't about giving a reason for your behaviour, and letting it continue unchecked. Self-awareness prompts you to be aware of it, so that you can start to take a bit more charge in how you are showing up.

You are a leader, after all.

When you are in the general practice of self-awareness, you are more able to give yourself what you need in that moment. Not to 'fix' everything, or make any experience necessarily go away, but to give yourself what you need *next*. This self-awareness will naturally ebb and flow between different degrees of awareness depending on a whole multitude of factors that can influence our experience. This is why it's a practice. The more you are in the practice of self-awareness, generally the quicker your response, or uptake, time is. Even if it isn't immediate, you might notice your shallow breathing patterns a lot sooner than continuing on indefinitely unaware of them.

Before learning how to practise self-awareness more intentionally, a CEO named Felicity (name changed) was constantly feeling on edge and frustrated with other people in her workplace. She had put it down to their overreach of their roles, which led to gaps – due to neglect of their own roles – being left in important areas of the organisation. Felicity's natural response was to work longer hours in order to make up for the oversight of fellow team members. Her role as CEO already involved extensive travel, so Felicity was feeling exhausted and annoyed. It became a pattern she was stuck in, and that others in the organisation had also become stuck in as a result; her pattern of behaviour had become a norm that people unconsciously came to expect. This unspoken expectation only exacerbated the behaviours from others that were driving Felicity's response to overwork to attempt to make up the deficits in the first place. She wasn't even happier as a result of all of this. When we started working together, and Felicity began putting some of these mindfulness practices into place, she also began to recognise just how stressed and overwhelmed she was. In addition to that, she started noticing when those feelings of overwhelm and agitation were much louder, eventually then connecting it to certain activities, conversations, or thoughts about the workload. This self-awareness helped Felicity put into place practices that helped her ease back from the overwork, ***and*** it also helped her step back from overreaching, and more into managing her team with more effectiveness; focusing more on her leadership role in managing her team members, including helping her team member – and herself – back into responsibility for their own role. This meant she could free up her own time and energy again, once those tasks were back with their rightful owner.

Another leader, Managing Director Christian (name changed), was struggling with his guilt over struggling at work. Christian believed that, as a leader, having a hard time mentally or emotionally meant he was failing in his role. He felt guilt for not being the picture-perfect, 'strong' leader he imagined for his team, further believing that him getting any kind of support meant he didn't care about support for his team, rendering him this image of the most selfish version of himself. This led to him withdrawing even more from his team, afraid to have them see any sign of what he perceived as weakness. This withdrawal resulted in his team feeling disconnected from and neglected by him, and in some instances unable to follow through completely on their own work, as they awaited notes from him that became harder and harder to access. When we got to work on his self-awareness and mindfulness practices, he could see more of the true impact of his actions. While he didn't intend on this impact, putting these practices into place helped Christian realise more of what he did need in order to accept some thoughts and emotions around work he had been experiencing. He was then able to have better conversations with his team members that actually helped alleviate the guilt he had built up and resulted in Christian's team members feeling more satisfied again with their own work and productivity.

Both Felicity's and Christian's scenarios have similar through lines, even though their experiences, feelings, and motivations differed greatly from each other. Both were experiencing a version of their work they weren't satisfied with but were based on misunderstood origins. Both of these experiences were also sending unintended messages to their team around them, which impacted the behaviours and satisfaction levels of those people. Both realised more about what they really needed, so were able to implement different practices or measures as a result of these realisations, which gave clarity and a better result to the team dynamics. By putting more self-awareness into place, that also involved measures that supported them through their stresses, each leader becoming more of the leader their team needed. What could be seen as a selfish act served them in a way which directly went on to serve the experience of those they lead.

This self-awareness, of course, speaks to your own personal stressors. It is also critical as a leader to understand your values, patterns of thought, and subsequent behaviour, and what triggers you. Exploring your patterns of thought supports more authentic, adaptive, and effective leadership on your part; arguably allowing for more job satisfaction for yourself while you're at it. This is because sometimes your thought patterns are conditioned by external expectations or your own experiences. Without conscious awareness of the possible conditioning, it is harder to have your thought patterns operating from your values.

Having the awareness of your values informs then how you lead, how you make decisions, and how you choose to interact with others, particularly in moments of disagreement.

Is Self-Awareness the Cornerstone of Emotional Intelligence?

Understanding self-awareness assists you in understanding how self-awareness underpins other domains of emotional intelligence: self-regulation, motivation, empathy, and social skills.

Daniel Goleman (Cherniss et al., 2006) emphasises that self-awareness is the cornerstone of emotional intelligence because it allows individuals to know their strengths and limitations, and to maintain a realistic self-assessment. Goleman's model of emotional intelligence is a prominent framework that emphasises four key components. These are categorised into personal and social competencies that allow any of us to naturally build each one upon the previous. These categories are: emotional self-awareness, self-regulation, social awareness, and relationship management. This model has been key in the formation of our collective understanding of emotional intelligence, and in how we can then apply it not only in our professional lives but also in our personal lives and experiences. In most academically robust models of emotional intelligence, self-awareness is at the beginning. We can take this as a reliable sign that what comes next relies on the foundation of our self-awareness. Without this, the rest remain largely insubstantial in impact; so if you're looking for an efficient way to implement emotional intelligence? The only way there is through.

Most people tend to think self-awareness is just about things that help us save face in potentially embarrassing moments, or being more about a gap in our skills or experience we may need – or want – to fill in. Self-awareness comes in more than just a one-dimensional form. Self-awareness can be distinguished between two different forms: internal self-awareness, related to knowing your values, emotions, and impact, and external self-awareness, which relates more to understanding how others perceive you. What is also important to consider and remember as you begin, or continue, to explore your own self-awareness is that these two forms are largely independent of each other; in that being high in intelligence in one form does not automatically equal competency in the other (Eurich, 2018).

Internal self-awareness and the continual practice of it allow you to get to know yourself more authentically. It can be confronting at times, perhaps when you realise where a particular reaction is coming from, that you even have a preference for something you believed you had never really thought about, or are feeling a certain way you were convinced – by all of the distractions – wasn't actually possible. While sometimes confronting and often uncomfortable, improving your inner self-awareness can help you recognise your own strengths and merits, as well as your weaknesses and areas for growth or improvement. Without self-awareness, it becomes really challenging to recognise the value you bring to a role, for example, when entering a yearly salary review conversation. It also makes it challenging to know where you could put more effort and energy into upskilling yourself when your self-awareness is lacking. As leaders, being continually teachable is important to our ability to continue communicating, making informed, educated decisions, and being an adequate leader to those we work with and around.

Having a healthy sense of self-awareness also means that you can more proactively align your actions closer to your core values. Consider how your decision-making and response process operates without this element in play. Without this kind of awareness, your responses and decisions are at more risk of being based on old habits or momentary, short-term ease, for the path of – seemingly – least resistance, rather than towards outcomes that you actually want and value. Just like being clearer in your values helps assist you in actually aligning with those values, since you have brought awareness to them and put them in the spotlight, the practice of self-awareness helps you to more easily recognise what is out of alignment with those values. Similarly, when it comes to working towards goals, be they personal or professional, awareness can inform you of how you are behaving, responding, feeling, or showing up in yourself, in relation to those goals, which is valuable information for you regarding aspects of yourself or circumstances that would be helpful to address.

External self-awareness helps us to be aware of how we are being perceived, or *could* be perceived, by those around us. None of us are expected to be mind-readers and know, absolutely, what other people see us as or what they think about us. But external self-awareness helps us to possess the recognition of possibilities; we are not trying – or able – to control what others think about us, nor should we, but it does assist us in coming to terms with what might be likely. For example, when it comes to leading, it is easy to feel and become more and more disconnected from the people you lead and support simply by being in the leadership position. It is not up to any of us to try to manipulate this otherwise, but being aware of this plays a role in how we might then choose to communicate or connect, and our own expectations for those connections as a leader. A CEO who has the self-awareness of the reality of a situation that they are either the owner or at the very head of a business can save themselves – and ultimately, everyone they work with – the added stress of the awkwardness, confusion, or energy expended that can happen if they attempt to build these important relationships without the awareness of how that dynamic might feel to the other person. Power dynamics are always in play in workplaces between leaders and those they lead, regardless of the quality of the relationship.

It's a reminder that each person in a workplace is just as valuable and deserving of respect and acknowledgement, and C-Suite to mid-level leaders do not automatically deserve more respect simply because of their title; but it's important to still be aware of that dynamic in leading and building relationships. A leader who wants to just be everyone's friend without the awareness of the responsibility of their role can make it really confusing for their team members if they turn around and show their 'management side' apropos of nothing other than an attempt to 'do' leadership. Having an awareness of the position you hold, in this example, helps you to develop healthier relationships, and even friendships where appropriate. Leaders set the emotional tone and, without self-awareness, they risk misjudging and misrepresenting situations unconsciously. This risks not only derailing or weakening teams as a result of unconscious factors, but weakening your impact as a leader too.

Naturally, this serves you professionally just as much as in your personal life. Professional leadership aside, this is relevant wherever you have relationships, including the relationship you have with yourself. Regulation of your nervous system isn't explicitly the goal, given that our ability to respond requires an element of stimulus in some way; rather, the goal is to continually be in a better relationship with ourselves and the experience, regardless of our level of regulation or dysregulation. You don't need to love it, or even want it to hang around, in order to improve your relationship with it. But that relationship, plus your awareness, is what enables you to respond to it in the first place. You can't begin to purposefully regulate what you're not aware of.

In leadership, and even regardless of leadership in life, a person who notices frustration rising is a person who can choose more deliberately how they want to respond and act on it, rather than reacting impulsively. Notice the distinction of experience here: you will, or may, have a certain kind of reaction. But when you are more aware of the feeling or sensation presenting itself, you give yourself more opportunity to still choose your response. Otherwise our world, and our world's leadership, would be held hostage to the whims of everyone's reaction based on their hurt feelings and egos.

Supporting Your Brain to Support You

The prefrontal cortex of our brain is the part that handles the regulation of emotions. Researchers have explored the role the prefrontal cortex plays in the early detection (awareness) and assessment of emotional stimuli prior to the behaviour 'reaction' being enacted. Put more simply for those of us who are not neuroscientists: there is evidence to show that practising mindfulness and deliberately cultivating self-awareness can strengthen the regulatory functions of the prefrontal cortex of our brain, which can lead to a reduction in reactivity, increased emotional resilience, and more flexible regulation strategies that help individuals manage their emotions more effectively (Dixon et al., 2017). What does this mean in our real-life application, whether as a leader or in more personal areas of our lives? These mindfulness practices that help you to develop and continue to practise self-awareness ongoing, help to develop the part of your brain that allows you to detect emotional stimuli earlier, giving you a good chance to appraise it for what it is before the reaction takes over. This can then lead to greater control over your emotional responses. It gives you an opportunity to consciously choose how you would like to respond, regardless of if your reaction is telling you to behave differently. When you choose how you would like to respond, you get to choose the course of action that steps in the direction you actually want overall.

While there are a great many reactions that might feel satisfying in the moment to act out – perhaps showing your frustration for someone cutting you off in traffic, or making a snarky remark to someone at work who seems to forget to bring their own pen to every meeting, or responding to that stranger online in the comments as if they are a direct adversary of yours – these reactions actually are not always going to help us in the direction that we really want the situation or circumstance to be heading in. They may feel satisfying and like you got one over on the inconvenience (person or otherwise), but not all of them actually progress you in the direction of the solution you want. This may seem like a simple and obvious concept, but it is also something that is easy for any of us to forget when we are caught up in the 'right' moment, with enough multiple layers of other stressors impacting how we are feeling. And while acknowledging those stresses or our emotions can feel confronting, we are likely to be impacted by them regardless of whether we acknowledge them – so we may as well give ourselves a chance to choose those responses as often as possible. Many of these reactions may give us that satisfying experience in the moment, but just as quickly as they happen, they can also push us in the opposite direction. Instead of working towards what we wanted in the first place, or where we ultimately wanted us or the situation to end up, they can distract and derail us instead.

Consider you are the person in the car, trying really hard to get somewhere important on time, and maybe you are feeling pretty stressed about the traffic. Then, somebody rudely cuts you off, maybe even with a particular kind of hand gesture. You, in the car, are now feeling extra stressed, and even surprised and a little angry at the car cutting you off, and you want to react and give them a taste of their own medicine. So in a single quick decision, you change lanes to get around them, and still in the reaction choose to cut off the original offender. Instead, this time, your heightened emotions and annoyance made you turn the wheel a little harder than necessary to change lanes in front of this person and your two cars end up colliding. This crash has now stopped you entirely, as well as the flow of traffic around you which is now compounding onto the stressful experience with everyone else's frustration. And you are stuck there, forcibly stopped from being on your way to where you were headed in the first place; only this time, you are not actually sure *when* you will make it, or if you can even make it in your car now. Not only that, you might now have the additional stress of the costs involved as a result of your reaction, as well as how it might impact the rest of your work week. Not fun, and definitely not useful. While this example might be extreme and you might find it quite a simple concept to resist the intrusive thought and decidedly not literally turn your car into a traffic jam, it makes that thought process and reactionary decision-making much easier to visualise and remember. In many day-to-day examples, it can be far more subtle of an experience. It could be as subtle or simple as the urge to suggest the person who always fails to bring a pen to the meetings is a bit silly and useless, passing it off as a joking gesture. But this gesture can actually damage the foundation of the relationship and culture if done enough times, instead of choosing to either accept it for what it is and leave it, or – better yet – choose to take the easy action of bringing an extra pen should anyone need it, which might actually make their life a bit easier. This gesture which can then inadvertently create a deeper sense of trust and camaraderie, opening up unexpected avenues of collaboration and progress; all from a simple act.

The prefrontal cortex has this early appraisal and detection capability that allows it to then influence how emotions are experienced, and then *whether* they lead to action. Of note, it does not function to cause us to not experience emotions at all. It does not switch off our ability to feel emotions, and a healthy functioning of our prefrontal cortex does not mean that switching off our emotions is the goal at all. What we are learning to do, little by little, better and better, is to be in a healthier relationship *with* our emotions. To be better able to acknowledge our emotions *and* still make a choice as to how we act, even with those emotions. All with the help of our prefrontal cortex, which operates as a bit of a gatekeeper in this emotions management. In an ideal scenario, it recognises emotional signals quickly, and then engages regulatory mechanisms that help to influence *whether* we act on these emotions, and in which case, *when* and *how* that action will happen (Dixon et al., 2017). It is doing a lot of work for us in the background, even as it continues and is still developing for all of us up until our mid-20s. Our brains work so intelligently in these ways we don't even know and almost cannot even be aware of as we go about our day. These practices of mindfulness and self-awareness are really practices to help our brain recognise more of those regulatory options should it need to in the moment. We practise things so that they become easier to access without the same effort. Basketballers practise free throws devotionally; what is typically seen as one of the most basic shots to the rest of us, is what many professional players focus on the most. Not the fancy three pointers, or the ones they get as they twist around an opponent player. That comes with practise in the game and in training. But free throws are the ones they ensure really land in their body, almost bypassing cognitive thought. This is so that when those opportunities arise, they are not taken by surprise in any way – especially for what is seen as such a simple opportunity to get points. This is so that when they step up to the line, they are not learning the feeling of it for the first time while under the stress and pressure of hundreds (sometimes millions) of sets of eyes on them while they go through the process. Self-awareness can sometimes have that feeling of those hundreds of eyes on us, simply in going through our own process of reflecting and enquiring inward. Even if there is, in a literal sense, nobody there to witness our own introspection, it can come with the same feeling of confrontation as if there were. When we practise it, it becomes more familiar to our own senses and experience. Practising these things helps that part of our brain – our prefrontal cortex – to better monitor and recognise our internal emotional states, so that it can help us to better respond to our experience as needed. This allows us to experience more adaptive emotional responses and regulation, than impulsive emotional reactions. Not for only in our personal lives, which can have an untold amount of stressors and emotional experiences that can feel overwhelming, but also for in our work lives and leadership, where often the personal can creep in and compile onto the pressures that we might experience in our roles, and the additional load of leading, guiding, providing valuable client or customer service, and supporting others within our team.

One important thing to remember here is that we are each of us human. This humanity means at times, even when we are trying to be mindful, we *will* make mistakes. Even when we are trying. Even when we have put all of the foreseeable measures into place to mitigate and avoid mistakes. You might choose to say something, thinking it is what is best and most useful, only to immediately recognise the mistake and even maybe feel a little bad about it the moment the words leave your mouth. Whether that experience is guilt, shame, or regret, it can be enough to affect how you experience the situation, in addition to your awareness of how it might be making someone else experience the situation. This is where, and why, repairing and the ability to repair become so important.

We as leaders must have the self-awareness to recognise when these mistake moments occur, and the mindfulness to both self-correct and situation-correct. Sometimes that looks like a genuine apology, with an adjustment or a plan of how that behaviour will be different in future, from that point onwards. Sometimes that looks like acknowledgement of how you could have delivered something better, and asking the other person what they need. When you make a mistake as a leader, it is easy to bury it with shame or busy yourself avoiding it. Add this onto the lack of examples in leadership we have historically that normalise admitting fault or fallibility; this can be one of the more challenging aspects of leadership. Acknowledging a mistake, and then making the often vulnerable-feeling ask in some form or another that invites feedback in how you can improve can in itself be its own emotional-spiking experience, on top of what might have already been the initial dysregulating experience that started it all in the first place. The more you practise and work on these skills, the more your system and the parts of your brain that get involved functionally here can function to help you recover.

Being a leader is not about being perfect and only showing perfection. Being a leader is genuinely trying, and then how you repair when those attempts do not hit the mark – and they won't always. This is your prefrontal cortex at work even when you recognise the mistakes and regret too. It, like you, is always learning by doing, and sometimes that means going through that process of recognition in retrospect of the event.

The Reciprocal Loop of Empathy and Self-Awareness

Humans, in leadership or not, who are more aware of their emotional states, have a lot more opportunity to put that into the practice of being more aware of and sensitive to the emotional states of others. Empathy doesn't ask us to have the exact same lived experience as someone else, or to even understand why someone else might be feeling something the way they are, in order to work. Empathy simply *is* the practice of recognising, sometimes even listening, that someone else is having an experience, and acknowledging their experience. To simplify it, it's the difference between:

> I don't know why you're stressed about this task. It's easy just to get it done.
>
> Versus
>
> It sounds like you're stressed about this task. What do you need?

This acknowledgement is made even easier the more we have practice in acknowledging our own emotional or mental experiences, even if they are different from what we are witnessing in others. When we understand, through self-awareness and acknowledgement, the toll that something like stress, for example, can take on us, it is much easier to acknowledge that potential toll it can have on someone else. Just like any other human experience: grief, torment, excitement, satisfaction, pride, frustration, fear. The whole emotional spectrum is fairly universal. It is not exclusively able to be accessed by any single demographic or 'type'.

The circumstances can, and might be likely to, change. Particularly on the extreme scale. It might be challenging for some of us who have never experienced something such as the displacement of war to understand that feeling. However, the self-awareness of *not* being able to even relate to that felt experience can be enough for us to show and express empathy for somebody in that circumstance. The misconception of empathy continues to be the expectation or assumption that we must have our own lived experience of what someone else is going through in order to show them adequate empathy or compassion. It's at once a significant pressure and an often insurmountable condition we place upon ourselves. This kind of pressure weakens our own confidence and sense of capability. It also weakens our ability to form genuine connections and provide valuable everyday support to anyone around us.

The pressure we can put on ourselves to have all of the answers can make it so much easier for us to avoid reaching out in the first place, for fear that we get it wrong. This perception of what empathy is, is then vastly blown out of proportion from the much simpler version that provides so much value in every direction in relationships and interpersonal dynamics. When it is really this: the ability to recognise someone's experience, regardless of our own experience in relation to theirs, allows us to better understand each other and ourselves.

As a leader, this can contribute to your sense of satisfaction in your work. Being more attuned to the emotional states of others, based on your relationship with and awareness of yourself, can help you feel more helpful to those around you. Not only that, it can help you feel more of your desired capability in your role, helping to keep you more actively interested in your work, and potentially even reducing your risk of burnout when you feel like you are actively thriving and flourishing in your chosen field. Empathy allows you to improve your interpersonal relationships in the workplace, regardless of anyone else's position above, below or equal to yours. Self-aware leaders can differentiate better between their own emotions and the emotions of others. When you are going about your work life understanding whether certain words or tones, whether accurately perceived or misunderstood, are more likely to be based on a reflection of you, or a reflection of someone else's experience that you may not yet even understand, you reduce a lot of unnecessary stress and energy expenditure.

Reducing your tendency for projecting stories onto others around you based on emotions or experiences that are solely yours helps to make you an easier leader to be around and allows your team members to be in a better, healthier relationship with you. This leads to less energy spent on miscommunications, clarity-seeking, unnecessary or even the wrong work spent on projects, and the culture of tip-toeing around each other. This way everyone is more able to, first, get on with the job at hand in the most straightforward way possible, and secondly, have a better experience of their work and each other while they're doing so.

This goes the same for how you perceive the moods of others, too. If you are over-identifying with someone else's mood, or your perception of that mood, and taking it personally because you haven't engaged your use of self-awareness that helps you to recognise that not all moods you experience from others are about you, you are only contributing to your own unhappiness. And perhaps even the other person's discontent, if you engage in the vicious cycle of avoiding self-reflection and clear communication, and react where you, as a leader, could instead choose to respond. Leadership means somebody must choose to go first, so it is not enough to continually rely on the expectation that somebody else will; sometimes that will even be in relation to how you relate with your own leadership or management team, and is especially important for how you relate to those you lead too.

Aligning Values with Leadership Actions

From Autopilot to Intentional Action

This is how self-awareness helps leaders shift from reactive to responsive leadership.

Values can be a tough concept to pin down. What might be perceived as a mission statement on the wall does not do a lot to demonstrate exactly *how* those values look in action in the context of the environment in which we mean them to exist. These mission statement-type declarations also do not always show at face value why we have chosen those particular values in the first place. As a leader, you are in charge of ensuring your values and the values you sow the seeds of into the workplace for those around you are clear and replicable. You want to ensure your team members understand what you stand for, and in order to do that, you must understand that in and for yourself first.

Research concludes that values-based leadership is not just idealistic but a pragmatic approach that underpins organisational excellence and sustainability (Žydžiūnaitė, 2018). This same study found that leadership that communicates values clearly and exemplifies them in real-life action on a day-to-day basis fosters more organisational alignment and employee engagement. It seems like a simple concept: find people for your team who value the same things you do and you will thrive. But when it comes to how *you* show up as a leader, there is nothing like the stress of the job or the day to dissolve that ease and desire for aligning with your values. This is where self-awareness and being mindful play an important role.

When you take the time to be aware of what you value in your work, in your leadership style, and what you desire to bring to the table, it becomes a lot easier for you to then align your actions with those values. Not only can you plan more in alignment, but it lessens the mental and decision-making load in the moment too. For example, if you receive some unexpected piece of information about a client or from a team member, if you are already clear and proactive in your values, you have already lessened the amount of mental sifting you must do to decide how you will choose to respond to the new information. You already know what is important to you in how you show up, so your mind can go straight to possible actions that align with that. If you are not clear in your values, or have not proactively paid them any attention, there is a lot more your brain has to work through as a part of the decision-making process in this new moment of time with this new information. Over time, that gets mentally exhausting and – very pragmatically – you become a less efficient leader; both of which can impact your wellbeing and how you feel about your work. Self-awareness and mindfulness are fundamental components of leadership, critical for leaders to intentionally align your actions with your moral values. This is as well as recognising your influence on those you lead and work with, and foster authentic and ethical decision-making more aligned with the culture you are actually wanting to support (Copeland, 2014).

As a leader who communicates organisational values clearly through actions, you play a role in setting the tone for the entire group of people you work with. These actions are less about what you say – or preach about – regarding your values or the kind of environment and culture you are trying to create. While communication is a very important skill to develop in leadership and workplaces, what is more important is how you demonstrate your values through your behaviour. Without the aligning behaviour, words eventually become empty and risk disenchanting your team; and often yourself along with it.

There are key principles that define values-based leadership (Žydžiūnaitė, 2018) that can be utilised as a guide to exploring your own values in relation to your leadership style.

Self-reflection: Leaders must reflect regularly and honestly with themselves in relation to their core values, what they stand for, why it matters to them, and how that looks in action.

Balance: It is a must for leaders to maintain a balanced perspective and be able to see situations from a variety of viewpoints outside of their own, in order to integrate all considerations into their decision-making process. This skill needs to be practised at every reasonable opportunity.

True self-confidence: When your values are based on your authentic character, and not superficially driven in relation to your ideal of success, it fosters trust and integrity; both with yourself, as well as how it reflects back from your team.

Genuine humility: Leaders should be able to recognise their limitations, value those around them, and demonstrate their role with humility. This includes remembering that you are human and are learning just as much as you are teaching others.

These principles collectively emphasise the *how* of carrying yourself as a values-based leader. What it shows most clearly is really the principle of living your values visibly through daily actions and by serving as a role model for others. Your interactions, when rooted in shared values, help you build authentic trust and relationships that foster a high-performance culture within your organisation.

Why Bother with Values in Leadership?

Some leaders are bound to ask why they should bother with values in leadership for the benefit of others. People are hired to do a job and get paid in return for that job, so why is it up to leaders or business owners to go the extra mile, or what we perceive as extra to what is simply necessary in relation to the job role? Traditionally, this arrangement of exchange has been seen as enough, so leaders can struggle with understanding why they need to place this extra effort upon themselves for others.

As society has changed, geo-political climates continue to create additional stress worldwide. Economic changes have shifted home lives, creating the need to work more for the same amount where income rates have not kept up with the pace of inflation, and gender roles – and subsequent legislation in some cases – have evolved to allow for more freedom of choice for people, particularly women, when it comes to deciding whether they want to have a career and cultivate what that looks like for them. Economically, this choice has also been taken away from many families where it is no longer possible to get by as a single income household while one person stays home. This all contributes to people's attitudes at work shifting, where what we value most highly is no longer the longevity-for-eventual-retirement benefits that were promised in days gone by, and is instead aligning more with what we can sum up as a more prominent desire for a quality of life and satisfaction of work. Besides these factors, we also know a lot more about wellbeing in recent decades than we ever have, particularly in relation to the impacts workplaces have on wellbeing, as well as the impacts of wellbeing practices on workplaces.

There is a broad scope of research into the benefits that values-based leadership and congruent leadership have on teams, organisations, and workplaces – including the people that exist within these entities. For example, Copeland (2014) explores how values-based leadership significantly influences employee perceptions and organisational effectiveness in multiple ways. Stanley (2008) also discusses the benefits of congruent leadership supporting the effectiveness of leaders when their actions consistently reflect the values they hold. In each case, these values-aligned congruent leadership approaches make those leaders more authentic and believable.

Leadership effectiveness: Leaders who demonstrate what are considered more moral, authentic, and ethical values are perceived as more effective by the people they lead. Other studies have shown that when leaders embody these values-based leadership behaviours, those they lead tend to view them as more credible and trustworthy, particularly in relation to behaviours such as integrity, fairness, and purpose. When it comes to congruence exhibited by leaders – that is, the meeting of action with what, or who, they say they are – this is found to positively influence how team members view and trust their leaders, which can reduce the delays that interpersonal friction can produce. This approach to leadership also helps to guide decision-making and behaviour (Žydžiūnaitė, 2018) more easily and frequently in alignment with values, where those values influence leaders' decisions and actions consistently.

Builds trust and credibility: A natural follow-on from leadership effectiveness is where trust is fostered more easily within organisations and teams, when values-based leadership and genuine, authentic attempts at practising congruent leadership are employed on the part of the leader. Because leaders' actions align consistently with their stated values and principles, it is naturally easier for team members, colleagues, and peers to believe in the integrity of those they work with. They more easily believe that their leader, in this case, means what they say and says what they mean more often than not.

Increased motivation and employee flourishing: Values-based and integrity-led leadership more actively supports employee wellbeing, which is a natural motivator within teams. When you consider the shared values that are more apparent when leaders are leading from those values, this creates more ease for employees to find where their own moral or ethical frameworks align with yours as their leader. This improvement in wellbeing, motivation, and enthusiastic commitment helps to support higher employee and team satisfaction, improving retention rates within teams. Additionally, from a bottom-line perspective, this approach to leadership is effectively a cost-saving measure for businesses. By making the extra effort for yourself and for your team members, you are saving your business, or boss, money while you work to improve the experience of those in your environment.

Improved adaptability and change management: When organisational and leadership values are clear and actions are in alignment with them, it allows for a more stable foundation for team members to adapt to change. Change is a natural occurrence in any business, regardless of whether it is the big, sweeping changes that can come along with organisational restructures, or the smaller, more day-to-day changes that occur, which can impact on a more individual level. Creating an environment that provides stability even in the midst of change as it occurs helps to improve trust and adaptability within teams and their members. This can improve stress levels, at least mitigating unnecessary stressors, potentially lessening the intensity of reaction experienced by either team members or leaders themselves.

A culture of ethics and integrity: When leaders lead from a place rooted in ethical values – whether that is through a specific values-based leadership practice, or mindfulness as a leader that makes you more aware of the integrity in how you show up in alignment with your values – it contributes to creating a culture where ethical behaviour is not only prioritised, but expected. This focus of leadership also assists in reducing the likelihood of unethical behaviours occurring, or being left unnoticed, in the first place. When ethical risks are more proactively mitigated through behaviours, it means less time spent on cleaning up messes, battling the fires that can come along with it, and dealing with issues that hinder team growth instead of supporting it. In turn, it means more time supporting improvements across all areas within the organisation, from interpersonal to job and business growth.

Improved organisational outcomes: Organisational cultures led by leaders who focus on practising more values-based congruence in their leadership and communication style often have a better reputation both within their own industry as well as with their stakeholders – both internal and external. It also begins to support a more sustainable, or even regenerative, culture that allows for better chances at longevity of success. Ethical practices, transparency as found in congruent leadership, and authentic engagement from leaders better ensure sustained success and long-term value creation, as well as responsible governance.

That is all to say, the benefits of practising more mindful, values-led leadership within your work go beyond simply the 'feel good' emotions. It comes down to this being a smart, even responsible, bottom-line supporting decision too as a business. This applies to any kind of leadership or industry; whether it is anywhere from Defence, to white-collar corporate, to creative, to investigative, and back again. A lot of what we know about mindful leadership, including living a life – in general – from a values-led place makes us feel better and more satisfied. In a way, it is almost a shame that even if and when we have the research to show it, that it still does not seem to be 'enough' for us – or businesses in particular – to prioritise without needing to understand the return on investment outcomes. Perhaps what is most notable in this discussion here is not even so much that there are financially and efficiency-beneficial elements, which certainly do make for an even stronger case for the use of values leading the way in how we ourselves lead. What is most notable is that despite countless lessons from poor values in leadership in history, it is still not comprehensively seen as enough to prioritise simply because 'people feel better when you lead this way'. When how we feel is so dismissed in the workplace, teams, and organisations, it makes it that much more challenging to prioritise. When it comes to values, it also makes it challenging to be in congruence with those values as leaders or business owners when the only, or main, motivation behind doing so is purely because it is so good for the bottom line.

Businesses do need to be financially successful in order to have longevity; there is no denying that. However, businesses run into trouble when values remain only about finances without prioritising the experience of the humans that make up that organisation. This sole focus can make leaders who profess to be 'values-led' feel off-putting and disingenuous, diminishing trust with the people they lead, and even their customers or client base; essentially anyone who works with or around them, or plays a stakeholder role in any capacity. The paradox being that even in their attempts to revive their leadership style or culture to something more aligned with values-led, focusing too much or solely on the financial benefits only risks doing further damage if that revival is felt or seen to be insincere. This is why education around the wellbeing and human benefits of values-led leadership, in addition to the other aspects we discuss in this book around mindfulness and emotional intelligence, is so much more important if it is to have the impact we desire. Understanding the benefits of the financial bottom line may be what gets you or this course of action through the door, particularly in environments where certain older styles of leadership are particularly entrenched. But the actual positive impact and having that return on the time investment relies upon shifting the narrative from 'this is how we win financially with this approach' to 'this *and* this is why we should care about how our people feel'. Full stop.

It is a delicate balance at times, and most leaders would say they do value how their people feel, and they likely would not be lying. There is a stigma inherent in how we talk about things like values, wellbeing, or even mental health, that can be met with that immediate, almost unintentional eye roll or scoff. People *know* that these things are important, but they are not always in touch with how that actually connects with actions, behaviours, words, policies, or tones. Many business owners and leaders will already actually have a list of their values, whichever direction they may exist in. But the question remains: Are you connected with those values as a course of action, in a real-world reality, or do they just sound good or look good on the wall to show how much of a 'serious business' you are?

Values Makes Things Easier, but the Path There?

Values work can be hard work even on a personal level. It is not often light-lifting and, like most else we speak of here, it requires a willingness to look internally. Really reflecting on your values can feel confronting, as you yourself are confronted with the realisation that there are values you feel you *should* have, that might not quite be the same as the values you are learning you *do* have. It can feel confronting to narrow it down; we are so often taught, especially in business, that we should try to be everything to everyone, be the 'everything' person to our employer or workplace. Even online in the never-ending news cycle, we are constantly under pressure to be across everything; everything happening right now, as well as the pressure to know everything that has ever happened historically, so that we can recognise immediately if an issue arises, or the context of something, or even who in the business world to avoid lest we be subject to the criticisms of everyone else. There is some truth to this in the sense that as members of society, we have a duty to not bury our heads in the sand. And yet, some things are simply not possible for us to have a fully informed opinion on, or be fully across the factual evidence. Values work prompts us to confront that pressure. If one of your values is social justice, or you have that neurodivergent leaning, this part may feel much louder to you. Regardless of why, there is often a type of reckoning we approach as we do this values work. It takes courage to say to yourself what you really place high in your top three to five values. It takes courage to narrow it down to only that many.

The argument for so few values that should be on our end list is due to exactly those themes we just explored; if we are trying to be and live up to everything, we cannot possibly do any of it well. Values are our guideposts that help us make decisions in alignment with what is important to us. If we say 'everything' is important to us because it seems simpler as an answer, we are actually making our lives so much harder trying to keep up with fulfilling it all. Not only that, we are also setting ourselves up for perpetual frustration and self-defeat when we can't live up to those ideals, and risk further disappointing and even alienating the people we serve in the process.

You need to build a relationship of mutual trust and respect between you and those you lead. This does not mean you need to be best friends with each other. Instead, this trust and respect support a robust relationship where there is a comfortable reliance and interdependency with each other. As a leader, if you try to prioritise as many values as you can in an attempt to relate to every single person possible, or please and appease, or to present the optics of doing the 'right' thing, you risk harming that relationship when you cannot possibly live up to all of them. It also risks harm when your attempts at certain values read more like you have copied them out of a book rather than truly feel and believe them in your body and in your actions. When everything is a priority, it's impossible to prioritise anything adequately.

Then you add business into this exploration and implementation of your values. Whether you own the business or not, the deep personal values work just becomes all that more visible. It can feel exposing and vulnerable, making you feel perhaps more risk-averse.

What if I try this or talk about my true values, and people tell me I am wrong? Or that I've missed one that should have made the list?

There is an immense amount of pressure leaders both have externally, and that they put on themselves. What you believe your values are can be informed by external pressures, and it is then up to you as a leader to do the self-awareness work determining some aspects about that response you have:

- Where is it my responsibility to assess and 'check myself' on why these values are not already a priority for me?
- Are my values in line with ethical leadership that reminds me I serve both myself and other people – whether as a leader or a business owner?
- Am I pretending that these are my values in order to appear more ethical or likeable?

We see this last point in particular present itself when it comes to *greenwashing*, where companies will either present a product, service, or themselves as an entity, or omit information about these, in order to be seen as better or less harmful to the environment than what they really are. This practice misrepresents the business to consumers, misleading consumers by enticing them to purchase or support the business under false grounds. This is an issue so much that the Australian Competition and Consumer Commission (ACCC) will investigate reports of greenwashing, which can result in financial penalties, as well as reputational damage and loss of consumer trust. This happens simply, or often not so simply, because a company has stated a value that their behaviour is not actually backing up.

One business owner continuously stated that two of their values were 'connection' and 'collaboration', even when we did the deep dive values work together. They had quite a people-focused business, where they were face to face with their clients every single day, often over long days. Connection as a value on the surface made sense by the nature of their business. Yet, whenever it came to real human connection, it was always experienced by others as very one-sided. Even down to the simplicity of polite and friendly greetings, this person would always answer 'and how are you?' with the same response: 'Fantastic'. While nobody is ever obliged to share their personal life in the workplace, and in some cases it is not always acceptable to, this rote response began to come off as insincere. How they behaved felt less to others like 'connection' and more like 'I read this in a book, and it told me how I should behave in order to make other people feel a certain way'. The difference between that advice and the outcome exists in that you need to mean what you say and how you behave, not just go through the process as if it's a strategy.

This person's clients and even their team members felt like it was more a method of control disguised as connection because the bids for connection were empty and lacked reciprocity. When team members attempted to genuinely offer collaborative ideas and perspectives based on their own unique areas of expertise, they were met with statements and decisions that felt less democratic to them than they had been led to believe the workplace system supported. They felt more dismissed and dictated to. Most business owners have the choice of how they want to run their business, and it is their prerogative if they want to be the sole decision-maker or ideas-generator; yet those with advisory committees, boards of directors, and a strong leadership team at the top indicate that success is found otherwise. Where this business owner made the mistake was attempting to align their values to something they were not aligning their behaviours with. They may have truly valued connection and collaboration but needed to then learn how to implement that in action; a common challenge many start-up business owners face when it comes to growing, expanding, and scaling their businesses. They eventually need to learn to let go of micro-managing every little thing in order to allow others to step into these areas of expertise so the business owner can step back and focus on the overall vision. On the other hand, it is possible that this business owner did not actually want the reality of a 'collaborative' environment where they truly 'connected' to those around them. In which case, it would have been more beneficial for them to cease attempting to push these values that were not actually in alignment with the reality they wanted. It might have created more trust with their team members, reducing the tension and frustration that comes with leaders saying one thing but then doing another. It might also have created more ease with clients, instead of leaving clients feeling shut out when they might have been expecting to feel a different sense of inclusion in that environment.

Authenticity and Harm – a Willingness to Learn

A lot of management advice – both in the research space as well as via lived experience – centred around leading with values comes from the attempt to encourage leaders to be more authentic. Like anything human-involved, it comes with nuance. It is important that you try to be authentic in your own leadership style so that you can build real, trustworthy relationships with those around you. It is also important as you do that to continue to avoid doing harm, especially in the name of 'just being authentic'.

This makes it challenging for both leaders and those who train leaders to find the balance; we don't want to dictate or micro-manage a person's thoughts. We do want to encourage continual learning and continued connection to the role of a leader; a role that is designed for encouragement and inclusivity. This can naturally butt against concepts or ways of being that have been instilled in us in our formative years. Just as social norms, and eventually laws and legislation, evolve, so must we as leaders. To do so is not a betrayal of you being inauthentic to who you are, but you leading and showing an authentic willingness to learn and do better.

At some – many – points in history, it was legal in many parts of the Western world to discriminate against Black or Indigenous people. In Australia, it was not until *The Commonwealth Electoral Act 1962* reached assent that First Nations people had the right to enrol to vote in Federal elections. Still not equitable, it took some time and a few years for each of the states and territories to grant that right within their own State-held elections. Even then, where enrolling to vote was compulsory for White Australians, it was not until 1984 that the *Commonwealth Electoral Amendment Act 1983* passed, granting First Nations people on par voting equality with the rest of Australia, making it now compulsory for all Australians to enrol to vote. Prior to this, between 1962 and 1984, it was simply an option of a right given. First Nations people were not treated equally to their White Australian counterparts in that time regarding voting, and yet it was technically legal.

It would be easy for leaders to convey their own authenticity according to the law and call it enough. Yet, those surface-level values do not particularly represent an authentic version of that leader. On one hand, it could represent that you truly agree with the inequities, which would continue to be a cause of concern for those around you. On the other hand, it could represent that your authenticity in this area went to the default standing without a deeper look or consideration into the impact it has on those around you, whether you lead them or not. This version of 'authenticity' might then present you as an uncaring or unthoughtful leader, which may inadvertently be at odds with your own values you have identified.

Leaders won't always get it right, but in order to be an effective leader with a positive impact, it is required of us to be proactive in assessing these kinds of values beyond, for example, what the law might say is a minimum standard. Being 'authentic' does not mean going by default; whether that default is legislation or perspectives you gained in your formative years that you have not re-evaluated since. This is like people who mistake 'just telling the truth' for allowing cruelty in their delivery. That is not authenticity, it's laziness.

Authenticity in your values work not only asks you to look at how your behaviours align with what you say you value, it also requires you to look at how your behaviours might present the direct opposite of the values you supposedly espouse.

Saying a word you value is not enough without looking at how your behaviour aligns, and more importantly, how it does not align. The reflection of this in a workplace, as an example, could be a leader waiting for it to be law in other capacities before they give First Nations, Black, or Brown team members equitable treatment. While anti-discrimination laws since are intended to put a stop to systemic racism within workplaces, there are still many instances within the private and public sector to this day that suggest otherwise. This reminds us that it is important to not necessarily wait for or rely upon what is in the legislation in order to improve upon how your own values manifest.

In another example, there is a female-owned and led Australian business now where the CEO and founder has taken it upon herself, as a leader and as a business, to offer to pay for the costs for any employee who wishes to seek diagnosis for Autism Spectrum Disorder (ASD) or Attention-Deficit Hyperactivity Disorder (ADHD). ADHD and ASD can impact how a person works best, their health and wellbeing, and their needs in order to thrive; and when those needs are not considered or met, it can lead to burnout and exacerbate chronic health conditions. At the time of writing, there is no law or legislation that asks a business or a leader to consider neurodivergence in their workforce quite like this, not least taking it upon the business to cover the costs of what is currently an expensive process. And yet, this leader is clear in her values of supporting her team in the ways they need in order for them to then contribute and thrive in their role – and their own lives. She chose this policy anyway, in a way that she could, because it was an actionable representation of her authentic values. Before they were in the financial position to offer this, she had other accommodations and supports in place within her culture. This leader created this culture because she led from that place, hired value-aligned employees along the way, and recognised in herself and within the team if and when that was falling short of that value.

While it is easy to presume that she would encourage legislation that helped to meaningfully support neurodivergent employees more, this leader did not default to just what the law said before she implemented a structure that supported her values. Unlike discrimination and harassment, it does not break any laws to put structures in place that improve quality of life at work in alignment with those values. As a leader, it is always put to you to be morally ethical, not (just) lawfully so.

Your Mindfulness Management Plan

Wellbeing itself can be a very subjective field of study, even when it's on yourself. While we have a lot of research into the field of wellbeing, mindfulness, emotional intelligence, and positive psychology – and continue to gather more – there is one common theme across it all: Even the most evidence-robust interventions, practices, and methodologies will potentially provide differing results when applied, depending on the human it is being applied to. That is the very nature of our brains – no two brains are exactly the same, so one application could still be as successful as another, but it might present very differently.

In leadership, this alone is a useful reminder. When leaders attempt to apply a 'one size fits all' approach to their team, it is normal to have varying results return to them, but those results are not always what they expect. Many high-performance leaders equate 'high pressure' with the expectations of high performance, which can mean they might set their team, or at least some of that team, up to fail simply by refusing to allow for the differences in the brains involved; which means different ways of thinking, different motivations, different backgrounds, different possibilities. It is all so variable. It is unfortunate that by many leaders, this has historically typically been viewed as 'too different to bother with'. It could be one reason wellbeing and mindfulness have previously not been as prioritised in the workplace and in leadership. We know a lot more about it now than we did even in the early part of the century, with positive psychology itself not really emerging as an academic field until the late 1990s. Even the concept of mindfulness has often more anecdotally been considered unnecessary and unrealistic to business until more recent years. Despite gaining more awareness and popularity in the business world for all the benefits it offers, it can still take a bit more convincing effort when it comes to actually applying it in practical ways.

It is just as important to avoid falling into this mistake when it comes to approaching mindfulness for yourself. As a leader, it is highly likely you feel pressure to get it 'right' the first time, or to treat your mindfulness as a performance – whether that pressure is coming from yourself internally, or from external factors or people. What is most needed for you to experience the benefits, almost side effects, of a mindfulness approach to your leadership is ironically, an element of self-awareness that allows you to meet your current needs exactly where they are and work from there. This is what will allow you to explore the different approaches openly enough in order to actually reap the benefits; not simply trying one, seeing it not quite fit, subsequently deeming it a failure, and going back to the same cycle that you were trying to get unstuck from to begin with.

Many people focus on prioritising an all-in, perfectionistic approach to mindfulness – if and when they do even approach it – that makes it appear to be more of a body or mindset 'hack', a fad that is driven by optics and an 'only one way to do it' mentality. These approaches can be damaging because they weaken confidence in one's own experience of their practice if they continually feel like they are doing it wrong. It also limits accessibility that is necessary for ensuring the practice is actually available for everyone, should they want it, in a way that they might need. When mindfulness becomes a performative talent show based on gurus and external pressure to be seen to be performing it correctly in order to satiate people other than the self, it greatly diminishes its value and impact. We, as leaders, can lead by example, share our experiences, and for those whose business it is, teach it. But we damage our own wellbeing benefits by placing unnecessary pressure on others to perform, for the perception of it all.

As a leader, this is why it is imperative that your mindfulness practice begins with you. Leaders are meant to go first when there is a choice given. While we can all lead and set an example for those around us regardless of our job title, rank, or standing, leaders are in that position for that particular purpose. For this reason, your own mindfulness practice can speak volumes and give valuable permission without you having to say much, or anything at all, about it.

Giving Permission

As a leader of a team, how you take care of yourself naturally reflects on those around you – much like it does for parents and caregivers with their children. People are always noticing the standards you set for yourself, whether or not they consciously recognise it. Something as simple and benign as always having lunch at your desk, for example, sets the example to your team that that is the expectation and standard you are setting. Before you know it, your team or workplace has a culture of never actually leaving their desks or having a screen break. Meanwhile, they are focusing on the stress of burnout, and you on the stress of a reduction in productivity or higher staff absenteeism or turnover. This has us moving backwards, when it is well known by now that we absolutely need breaks in our day, not to mention the legislative requirements of managers and business owners to ensure their staff take their breaks.

Mindfulness can be about these everyday, seemingly simple yet often overlooked habits. It is also about the deliberate actions and practices you might employ for yourself as additional support. These are practices that go beyond what is more obviously in your job description. These are the things that others may or may not know you are doing, but still may be aware of the noticeable difference in you. For example, you might begin a new practice of creating the habit of ensuring you have some time to yourself in the mornings before work, whether that is by way of a morning walk or workout, screen-free time with your dog over a proper breakfast, a breathing or meditation practice, or something else that appeals to you. The people you work with or manage might not know this detail about you and your habits outside of work, unless you share it, but they are still possibly going to notice the difference in you as a result. Maybe that difference is how you enter the office – in person or virtually – each morning; where before perhaps there was an air of stress, as you frantically rushed into your day, over time they might sense or be able to see more outright a sense of ease, clarity, and flow. This then can set the tone further for the day, for you, and for the people around you. Calmer leaders calm others.

We will get more into the specifics in the next chapter, where we will outline more of the details, the how-tos, and the benefits that have been indicated in the research. What is most important to start with is this:

What can you do most consistently, not necessarily for the longest at a time?

It's an easy mistake to make. We might feel so excited by learning this new thing, or feel so much relief from having applied or experienced it so far, that we want to go all in. So we set ourselves the goal of '30-minute sessions, every day', idealising this fantasy of how it will feel when we implement this into our routine. Until, that is, the rest of our realities start to creep in; perhaps we realise that the demands of having kids while everyone in the house is trying to get ready in the mornings don't really support this new habit we're attempting, or it's creating more anxiety than helping, because it feels like another significant chunk of time out of our calendar to navigate. Whatever the reason, in many cases 30 minutes can feel like a lot in our busy lives. So then you start to do it less and less often, maybe dropping down to once a week, then once a fortnight, and then more ad hoc when it's once whenever you remember. All of a sudden, you're not in the practice, and more in the feeling of catching up and even feeling like you've 'failed' at another thing that you always meant to do.

In scenarios like this, what is more effective than the occasional best attempt at a 30-minute practice, even if those attempts are noble, is actually a shorter practice more regularly. This can be as short as five minutes, or even as long as it takes to take five whole breaths, but something that you are more able to practice every, or most, days.

These are the same conversations I have had with soldiers during my time working with up to 50 soldiers at a time over a course of eight weeks for each programme, teaching them about how the nervous system works, their stress and the regulation and dysregulation that can happen, as well as taking them through practical and experiential mindfulness exercises to help them put it into tangible practice. Being a generally action-focused demographic, naturally the most common question that would be asked by the participants was one around 'what's the best time of day and length of time to practise mindfulness?' In this case, they were referring more specifically to mindfulness as more of a meditation practice itself, that would naturally then assist them to build more mindful habits throughout other aspects of their day.

They wanted a plan and, like many people, wanted the thing they could be told to do, so they could then take it with them. It's understandable to desire this. Part of the practice of mindfulness is being deliberate in our practice. Deliberate, intentional, and inquisitive. This means that part of the practice is reflecting on your own day, and exploring where you can make a practice fit in, noting that everyone – yourself as well as the people you work with and lead – will have different demands on their day. We do not all have the same 24 hours in our day, because each of us has different capacities, different systemic conditions, different home lives, different bank accounts, different brains, different abilities, including disabilities, and different desires.

All of this, and yet people can still put pressure on themselves in order to get it 'right'. But you cannot get it 'right' when you set the goalposts in an entirely unrealistic place in relation to your life; with the added pressure of life never changing, lest it impacts your ability to practise your mindfulness meditation for that same 30 or more minutes every day.

It's been said already, but it's worth reiterating: the best time and length of meditation is the one you can do most consistently. This answer requires you to be reflective about when that works best for you, in your current season of life. It also leaves the answer with you autonomously, and not another teacher or leader who you need to continually check in with at all times, for the rest of your life. Somebody could tell you that mornings are the best time, but if your mornings are already full with other things you are trying to fit in ahead of your day, and instead you could use that decompression at some point during or after your workday, that morning direction might not be best for you. It also does not allow you as much of that practice of self-awareness and autonomy to properly explore your own needs and reality for your practice. Instead, by looking into when might work most consistently for yourself, it encourages your active participation in the exploration of your mindfulness practice. It goes from something that someone else outside of you has instructed you to do, to something that you are actively taking part in for yourself. You now have more autonomy over how you schedule that into your – likely already busy schedule. This includes your ability to adjust on any given day where you might need to move things around. Our lives, and therefore our needs, are fluid and changeable.

Your mindfulness practice is not meant to be treated as separate from your life. It is meant to be practised as a part of it. This is part of what makes consistency one of the most important factors; it allows you the continuity of practice that assists you in integrating it. The other important factor that this allows follows on from that: continuity of practice. Practising something more regularly, even in shorter moments at a time, helps us to learn something a lot more effectively than some of those bigger blocks when they are inevitably spread further apart. Mindfulness should not be left as something that is accessible only to those in privileged positions who may have more time and space in their day to dedicate to it. Especially not when something as short as five minutes per day, consistently on most days, can be effective enough in bringing about positive change in your state of being regarding mindfulness.

Once the habit is built and you are more actively in the practice of even remembering to prioritise your practice – which can take some time, especially if conditions like autism or ADHD play a role in how you schedule and structure your day – you might like to explore extending that initial length of practice. Using the five-minute practice as an example, you might eventually want to explore extending your practice one day to a 10-minute practice, keeping the five minutes as your baseline. There is no limitation on how long you do extend your more regular practice for, if at all. That is up to you to discern. This section is simply intended to provide you with a guide to creating that foundation. When you ensure that you have a foundational baseline in your practice, in a way that is intentional for you, it can help to reduce the friction you experience in your practice. This is particularly useful when we consider that mindfulness practices will change over the course of your life, by nature of you changing over the seasons of your life. By being more in relationship with how you adapt your mindfulness to your day as you set these foundations, you are in the practice of being more able to respond with positive affect to adaptation in other areas of your life as it happens.

Boundaries Defining What Leadership Is, and Boundaries That Define Your Leadership

There are two focuses of boundaries to explore here. One is the boundaries that expand your definition of what leadership is. The second is the boundaries around habits and activities that enable you to be an effective leader. And they are both inextricably linked.

Much of what has defined traditional leadership is what now keeps us stuck in old structures, dynamics, and values that are limiting at best, and damaging at worst. Leaders are no longer as effective operating within the 'old ways', but like any change management, it can take a bit of exploration, preparation, planning, and plain and simple *work* to shift these paradigms. It begins with awareness. Expanding the bounds of what leadership development involves, to then cultivate a more inclusive and values-driven approach to leadership that is inherently more relational ultimately enhances that leader's effectiveness and outcomes within the team and organisation (Rocco & Davis, 2024). By first expanding your own potential pre-existing boundary of what you perceive to be 'traditional' leadership, and including in that development of a deeper understanding of yourself and others, you are more able to create, and further facilitate for those you lead, a culture that values deeper interpersonal connections between leaders and their team members, cultural sensitivity, and adaptability. Making you a more versatile and supportive leader, this approach that places self-awareness, values, and relational leadership as a valuable practice helps to shape and develop a more authentic organisational culture that is supported and demonstrated by you.

That is part of the boundaries work on you, but all of us collectively, in leadership: to stretch the boundaries of what leadership *was,* to what we now recognise it *is* moving forward where it is much more about the collective than it is about any single individual. Much like third wave positive psychology, where it is now exploring beyond the individualistic sense and more of the systems in which we exist and how these systems impact our wellbeing, our leadership must also acknowledge those previous barriers and expand. Our leadership must go beyond just focusing on the positive benefits for ourselves (first wave), or acknowledging and highlighting only our feelings, whether they are positive or negative (second wave), and must now explore the systems that we influence, impact and are impacted by, and encompass individual, organisational, and cultural dimensions, where our effectiveness as leaders is contingent upon these broader influences, now more than ever (Kiker & Callahan, 2019).

When we expand these bounds of what leadership really is there to function as, and for, we become far more effective and well – this time bringing along more of those around us, with us.

Boundaries in Practice

Dr Raquel Martin (Psychologist, Professor, and Author) helps us to define the distinction between a boundary, a rule, an expectation, and a standard. They work so seamlessly adjacent to each other that it can be very easy to overlap one into the other. Instead, consider that they work *in relationship* with each other, rather than operating in silos independent of one another.

- *A boundary:* Guides your behaviour, and your behaviour only. It clarifies what you are or are not willing to do, be party to, or receive. That last part of receiving is tricky, because often we want to turn around and make that about how others behave towards or around us. A boundary can only be set by ourselves, for ourselves. It may just be in relation to how we relate to others, as much as we relate to ourselves. But it must solely focus on our own autonomy in this moment.
- *A rule:* Tries to control someone else's behaviour. In certain workplace contexts, this can be fairly appropriate, particularly if it involves workplace health and safety, or considers creating a psychologically safe workplace – whether that is because legislation has dictated as much, or because it is something you value in addition to the legislation in place. If it is simply in relationship with another person where a seemingly arbitrary rule has been put into place, this could indicate a bleed from boundaries into the attempt to control someone else's behaviour in the name of 'a boundary'. In which case, refer back to the previous point.

- *An expectation:* Is what you hope others will do. Different from a rule in how enforceable it is, an expectation is a hope for a certain kind of behaviour. It could be as simple as the expectation that you hope someone close to you will ask how you are in return when in a conversation with them. There is no rule that says everyone has to go around enquiring into the wellbeing of everyone else around them, but in any kind of personal relationship with them, it could be *expected that* they would.
- *A* standard is what you allow in your life: This is what you allow for yourself, from yourself – your own behaviour, words, attention, and environment. Similar to a boundary, a standard is something *you* keep. In a workplace or other shared environments, it becomes slightly more complicated because each person will have their own standards. As a leader, where it is outside of rules or legislation in place, you naturally have more authority and visibility to set a certain standard. This is why your self-awareness and intentionality are important to practice; you are setting a standard, whether you recognise it or not.

What is important to remember is just because something may not fit into the definition of a boundary, does not mean that it is free of consequence if you or someone else breaks that rule, expectation or standard. Consequence, different from punishment, is not in place with the purpose to worsen someone else's position, but simply an outcome as a result of another thing.

The consequence of someone breaking a rule could be more legal or punitive in ways. Just like someone breaking the speed limit while driving is breaking a rule, they – and all road users – can reasonably *expect* that there would be a fine or other inconvenient consequence handed down when caught. In a workplace, a broken rule could cause anything from re-training to performance management to termination of employment.

The consequence of someone breaking an expectation you had for them, whether specifically or more in general as a human, could be a possibly uncomfortable conversation to clarify what felt missed in that moment as you or they attempt to repair to move forward. It could also be the consequence of the dynamic of the relationship shifting, not out of punishment necessarily, but in the connection of the interaction. In a workplace context, it is important not to use missed expectations as a punishment at the expense of the team or the work to be done; freezing someone out of valuable information they need in order to fulfil their duties in their role is closer to manipulation and sabotage than it is to being a natural consequence.

The consequence of a standard not being met first lies in self-reflection; that standard might have been missed by yourself, not just someone external to you. For example, where have you possibly let the standard slip of behaviour or language used? Just like many parents receive the reflection of the language they typically use when they notice their children beginning to use it, whether that is with more adult-appropriate words added to their vernacular, or how they learn to speak to others based on what has been modelled for them, it is not necessarily appropriate for punishment – particularly not until the adult in the equation self-reflects on where they let their standards slip that set a different example for those watching than intended. This humility, whether at home with young kids or in the workplace with peers and team members you are leading, is key to improving the standards. Leaders start first, which also means leaders check themselves first.

With supporting change for the individual or the group comes the work of what that actually looks like in practice. Like anything, part of implementing new behaviours, habits, or structures – such as in business – requires setting up some form of boundaries in order to give the appropriate amount of time, energy, and effort to making it happen. To become a more mindful leader, you need to give space in not just your own mind, but often in your calendar and the physical aspect of your day to practice it. You might find that your mindfulness practice – of both being more mindful, as well as doing more mindful things – will require the same, particularly in a professional setting. When it comes to the seemingly more 'productive' aspects of our roles that tend to have a more tangible, easily recognisable benefit that makes it easier to justify, scheduling your day to support those activities might come easier. However, with mindfulness, when it is something that is less tangible, particularly as something that when it produces results, those results are not as physically tactile or visible, it can be more challenging. This challenge can come in the form of the challenge to get any support needed in order to prioritise, as well as challenging to feel like you can justify your energy and attention to it. As a leader, you have more privilege and authority to help encourage these helpful practices and behaviours. So, like many other elements of your work, it might have to start with you.

Mindfulness practices come in many forms in the workplace. They could take the form of more specific meditation and mindfulness practices, regardless of whether this is during official work time and space. This can be made simply a part of the regular encouraging conversation or even accessible to employees via an Employee Assistance Programme (EAP) or similar employee programme offers. Mindfulness in the workplace almost more noticeably shows up in things like your deliberate use of language with others, inclusivity, equity of opportunity; both in apparent and systemic presentations.

Your deliberate use of language as a leader will play a significant role in shaping the environment in which you exist and, therefore, impact. Part of your mindfulness management plan must be around the language you use; internally with yourself, as well as externally with others. This goes beyond simply mindset, where a growth mindset can play a role in significantly positively impacting motivation, willingness to learn, and achievement. As a leader, you can set boundaries by way of how you choose to communicate; most pertinently while under stress.

First, let's begin with a comprehension of what boundaries in this context mean. There is some confusion around boundaries, with many feeling that the word is too harsh, assuming that it focuses more on pushing people away or existing as a punitive measure. Instead of considering boundaries as a punishment, let them be neutral, where there *may* be a consequence if they are not met, but that consequence is not necessarily punitive. It is simply an outcome based on the occurrence of 'something'.

It is more helpful for us to consider boundaries as a way of how we learn to be in a better relationship with ourselves, as well as with others. A boundary with, or for, yourself allows you to be in a better space to better take care of your needs so that you have more of what you need – capacity, energy, clarity, focus – in order to show up in the intentional way that you would like to. This is important as a leader. As an example, boundaries with or for yourself can look like disabling notifications for a set period of time you might have blocked out on your calendar in order to do deep focus work. Part of setting the boundary could also be to communicate that with your team, letting them know in this example that you will be unavailable for the next hour so you can focus – however, this can include clarity or stipulations on what would constitute a reasonable or necessary reason for interruption. This clarification can be helpful to help both you and your team members relax more into this boundary you have created. What this boundary then allows for you is time and space to focus on something that is important for you – or for your team or business – without the mentally draining aspect of task switching too often.

It creates the space for creativity, solutions, resolution, or simple productivity towards completion where, by the end of the set time or the task completion itself, you get to experience satisfaction in the progress as well as a feeling of accomplishment. Not only that, you have practised presence in a very tangible, real-world way.

What your team gets out of you having reasonable boundaries for yourself such as these is a leader who is more present and less distracted; a leader who is working on reducing their stressors in effective ways; a leader who has more attention and energy to give; a leader who understands through experience the usefulness of being able to focus on a sole task and minimise the need to task-switch often; a leader who hasn't unnecessarily stretched themselves beyond capacity across multiple things; a leader who is clearer and more coherent in how they communicate; and a leader who can lead all of this by example for their team members.

Boundaries with others are the complementary aspect that is important for a leader; they allow leaders to ensure that their work expands to those around them, rather than being an individualistic pursuit that only benefits themselves. When advice is given and discussions around boundaries are had, often it can be with this individualistic lens that places more effect and emphasis on the individual person than on society as a whole. How each person feels is indeed an individual and personal experience. The risk in this skew towards individualism, however, lies in a dismissal of or forgetting that how we behave and show up affects more than just us, and that there are systemic elements within society that historically and presently impact individuals, no matter how much 'self-improvement' they perform. We all benefit best when we integrate the two approaches. Otherwise, we run the risk of increasing our sense of isolation and disconnecting from much-needed community in the name of improving the self. On a personal level, it does not matter how much you eat 'well' – particularly if you name it as a boundary – if it cuts you off from even occasionally enjoying and sharing a meal with other humans around you. On a leadership level, it does not matter how much you set any boundaries for yourself; it cuts off access and connection with those within your team by refusing to share them. The risk lies in ultimately forgetting that leadership exists to benefit the whole, not just the person. When communicated clearly, boundaries can be a virtual step-by-step playbook for how we can be *better* in community and connection with others, including in the workplace or team environment, rather than in self-focused isolation, even if it has the intention of 'optimising' your results.

This is all to say that when approaching boundaries with others, it is important to keep in active consideration how they exist to serve the relationship, not act as an exclusionary agent to it. In a team setting, boundaries could look like how you choose to speak to one another, perhaps with you even leading or initiating a process if need be; this could be something simple and similar to 'what question do we ask first before we assume *this*?'

The boundaries you lead around mindfulness, and how that means you and your team communicate with each other, can make all the difference in how you function and grow as a team.

Boundaries around Tolerating Prejudice – Racism, Sexism, Ableism, and Discrimination in the Workplace

Aside from legal requirements in adherence to anti-discrimination laws, as leaders I suggest it is up to us to ensure we are leading morally and ethically, regardless of whether it is a set requirement 'legally'. If you are only leading to a certain standard because it is required legally, and not because you care about the experience of those you lead, there is more work for you to do in order to step into leadership. Depending on where you are, there is going to be at least some baseline of laws against discriminating in the workplace, whether that is around racism, sexism and misogyny, ableism, or any other form of discrimination that can show up. However, we know that leaders have the power to influence cultures that might technically adhere to these laws or guidelines, but still not create the experience of inclusivity and safety for the people who exist within the ecosystem of that culture.

Laws are one thing. Behaviour can show up differently and still be considered legal, so your leadership responsibilities do not end as far as they meet the law.

Boundaries as a leader are also important to how you lead through your behaviour, including the structural part of your mindfulness management plan as it pertains to your role in leading by example. Off-the-cuff comments about someone else could impact how safe someone within your organisation feels, depending on the tone and reasoning as to why you made the comment. Poor behaviour you let slide because someone is a 'good performer' in the workplace diminishes the quality of the workplace culture and can increase staff absenteeism and turnover, costing you even more money. Giving non-promotable tasks to only women, such as cleaning the kitchen or covering the phones at lunchtime even when their role is specifically not client-facing, may not seem outwardly discriminatory and may even be justified by 'how good they are at that task'. What it does is not only potentially harm the culture of the team but also suggest that, by the example of your own behaviour, those people and their contributions are less valuable than others; in this case, those women being tasked with non-promotable tasks and their time are less valuable than perhaps the men in the same environment, or even role, who could easily do those same tasks but simply are never burdened with such an ask or expectation.

Your attitude towards these trends will inform and influence the attitudes of those around you feel permitted to have, no matter how quiet you may be about it. What you allow quietly is what you permit loudly. The behaviour, trends, attitudes, and side comments people in your team feel emboldened to express are supported by your lack of willingness to hold boundaries around how the culture of the team is held by all.

Boundaries are important in how you lead, which is a structural part of your mindfulness management plan as it pertains to your actual role; not just as a leader, but as a colleague, peer, and participant within the organisational culture.

Developing Self-Awareness as a Lifelong Practice

Mindfulness practised by leaders can be beneficial in improving the psychological health of the individual, as well as the organisational health. This health includes advantages in increased resilience, emotional composure, and stress coping mechanisms. Leaders who cultivate self-awareness also drive engagement, organisational good citizenship, and high performance (Goleman & Cherniss 2024). When leaders are stressed, their people feel it. When leaders are grounded and present, even in high-stress moments, their people feel it. In each case, they respond accordingly.

The challenge in developing self-awareness as a lifelong practice is the more you need it, the less likely you're aware of your need for it. That is the illusion of self-awareness as a requirement – many think they have it and do it well, but few actually do (Eurich, 2018). You could follow the step-by-step of any guidebook or comprehensive list of suggested activities that help you develop more self-awareness and still not be any further along in your awareness if, for whatever reason, you're only approaching it as steps to do. But self-awareness is going to look different for each person, and have a different level of accessibility because of a variety of factors, some of which will include the state of their mental health, capacity and internal resources available, and the support they both feel and need. One person's 100-m sprint is another person's year-long mission. One person's ease into self-awareness is another person's confronting nightmare. So while there are some suggestions that can be provided as a guide to developing more self-awareness, this can only ever be a guide and may require more professional, psychological guidance and other adaptive measures at any point.

One important thing to remember over this lifelong journey is that your level of self-awareness will not all look the same or possess the same intensity every step of the way through. Perhaps one of the biggest challenges is that there is no particular level of achievement to be reached with it – just benefits you start to become aware of, sometimes in retrospect, as certain moments happen and you notice that you've handled them much differently to how you might have previously, or you're more able to clearly articulate your experience with ease, because you've already become aware of it and named it for yourself.

The lifelong practice is intended to remind you of exactly that: we will never perfect it, and our level of competency with self-awareness will ebb and flow over the course of time and life seasons. But we continue to practise it, so that maybe it becomes a little easier to bring ourselves back into it each time we need to, no matter how many times that ends up being.

The first step to this practice is to accept that it will be repeated over and over again, just like tying your shoelaces, having enough water each day, or brushing your teeth. It's a maintenance approach that must be treated as such.

Put Your Support Systems in Place

Sometimes we don't know what kind of support we need until we're in the thick of it. You also might not even be aware of some support available until someone else suggests it. One practical strategy is having support mechanisms in place that will help you with your practice. This might look like anything from having your schedule support you in helping you to build the habit and practice, to encouragement from key people in your personal life, to professional support-givers.

Different forms of professional support can present as a coach who can help you reflect, be accountable to your practice, and ask the right questions to help you actually be in the practice of self-awareness, rather than just ticking the box. Mental health professionals can also provide valuable support, particularly to help you navigate anything that the self-awareness practice or deeper reflections might bring up that requires adequate training. Once again, you may not be aware of what is there to come up until you are in the practice and process, so even having the support of people close around you to begin with can provide a valuable, supportive foundation for you to then grow on from there.

Explore Different Methodologies

Just like different modalities will work differently for different people, so too will they work differently for you depending on the season. Don't take it as a failure if one stops feeling as effective for you; take it as an opportunity to explore the experience of a different approach. It might also be useful to have a list of different practices on hand as a reminder, since some will be ones you sit down to do and others will be those you practice as you go about your day, interacting with yourself and others. These could be embodiment practices such as yoga, meditation, walking, surfing, dancing, or anything else that involves body-mind connection. They can also be activities such as journalling – which can take the form of appreciation journalling, reflecting on the day or an event, desire journalling, journalling out frustration by acknowledging the thoughts and feelings, or positive enquiry journalling where you explore in journal form how you are feeling in relation to a specific prompt from your body or day. Other modalities come in the form of reflective dialogue, which can be done by yourself or with someone else, and engaging in a coach to help guide you with the questions that you don't necessarily know to ask.

Other methodologies are more *in practice* in your day-to-day life: active listening, active enquiry into your own responses, regularly checking in to where you feel tension in your body throughout your busy workday, moments throughout your day with your own thoughts or experience without external stimuli influencing that, even if just for a minute or two at a time.

This is not a comprehensive list of all the practices or habits you can explore to develop more self-awareness, but they show the broad range that self-awareness practices can take form in that shows, once again, there is no one single *correct* way for this to work. It just requires you checking in, in whichever way you are able to or capable of, with consistency.

4 Empathy and Social Skills in Action

Empathy: The Bridge to Authentic Connections

Empathy is often mistaken for the experience of '*I must feel exactly how this other person feels, or know exactly how they feel, in order to show empathy*'. We have, inadvertently and in a variety of ways, somehow learned that it 'doesn't count' if we do not understand each other exactly. This could be part of the disconnection we can experience between us and other humans, between our social groups and other social groups, between those we recognise as 'us' and those we somehow see as 'other'. Waiting for yourself to feel exactly what someone else is experiencing before you can acknowledge and empathise with it is not empathy in practice. It is a common misunderstanding when empathy is often defined as the ability to share and understand the feelings of another, but the practice of empathy does not need you to share in the experience; it simply asks you to acknowledge it.

The *Black Summer* bushfires in Australia over the 2019/2020 fire season were amongst the worst, most literally devastating fires on record in Australia. With the proliferation of social media ensuring that our algorithms were set up for us to be exposed to a constant stream of footage of the devastation – from families fleeing homes and hiding out in nearby bodies of water awaiting rescue, to the sounds of animals caught up in the fires, to the vast devastation of local flora and fauna – it was hard for any of us tuned in not to feel the emotions of the experience, even if we were experiencing these things from the safety of fire-free zones. From the safety of the homes of those of us watching along online, it still felt heavy and sad. This acknowledgement of the devastation and how it might feel for those directly affected would fall under the description of empathy.

Where it stopped being empathy, and possibly more an experience of vicarious trauma at least in some cases, was when those who were safe and never were in any direct danger began to shut down as if they had been directly impacted themselves. Not the people who had perhaps family and friends impacted that they were concerned about, but others who felt and truly believed that to continue on with 'business as usual' was to dismiss the experience of those going through it. The danger in this being, particularly for small business

DOI: 10.4324/9781003632771-5

owners out of harm's or impact's way, if they were to stop what they were doing completely, their ability to help or support in meaningful ways is greatly diminished; most often because of the resulting reduced income. They then, in a different way, become a victim of the experience rather than an empathetic support for those in the primary experience of the devastation.

Being human is complicated and there is no rule book. Sometimes there will be times when the world feels heavy and people might not understand what we are doing it all for, even if we are not the ones being directly impacted by the destructive removal of civil and human rights, or the ongoing invasion of a country, or the most documented genocide and war crimes committed in history. There is no playbook on how to handle first the experience itself, and then handle the constant onslaught of information about the experience or event that, in many cases, is not simply a repetition of the same event but is a continuation of additional injustices over time. It is no wonder that people feel as affected as they do. But if we come back to the clarity of what empathy really is, as leaders it's helpful to keep in mind this differentiation as we carry out our roles and attempt to continue with our days. As a leader, your empathy could acknowledge that someone in your team – or even yourself included – is feeling agitated by the current events of the world. Empathy as a leader would acknowledge that.

The unhelpful approach would be mistaking the experience of living through one of those world events as something that you need to know the feeling of in order to then acknowledge. This is where we risk a complete lack of empathy as the pendulum swings in the other direction. This complete lack of empathy often sounds like *'Well I'm not affected, so it's not my problem'*. This often shows up as an issue in workplace considerations for people who have a different experience than you – whether that is disability, gender-related, mental health, or cultural. It has also many times sounded like confusion and dismissal over why a team member is upset that they are often interrupted or unacknowledged during meetings, or another is asking for considerations around prayer times during Ramadan. On a broader scale, this can impact voting choices and legislation; when voting citizens remain so focused on only improving their own circumstances without acknowledging that other people might be struggling with theirs, simply because *they* have not experienced that particular struggle themselves, it risks creating a more divisive society. This divisiveness can actually negatively impact quality of life even more than if we took considerations into account as a standard.

Two Truths Can Exist at Once

Outside of factual data, when it comes to emotional experiences, we are so often caught up in our own that we assume the experience of others is either the same or not as important as our own. This is shown in many visual perspective tests – where an image is designed in a way that you could see one of two different opposing images within the same image, where, for example, one perspective may be a duck and the other a woman holding a cigarette. These images, particularly when they go viral online, often end up in debate with people commenting at each other from across the world, '*of course the dress is blue and black, what do you mean it's white and gold?*' We know what we *know* because our experience says so, and in many cases, we call it that.

Where scientific and factual data is based on replicable studies that produce the same outcome, and science itself exists as a field to continually prove itself wrong so that we can continually learn more and *better* about those things which we study, emotional and personal experiences are much more challenging to assert definitively that *this* is the truth, and *that* is not. But we still try, often unconsciously and without an awareness of what we are doing. When we try to be empathetic and show empathy outwardly, often leaders will mix up the need to understand and see exactly why that person might experience what they do, with an actual display of empathy.

For example, you might have a team member who is displaying the signs of stress and overwhelm. Perhaps they are often appearing frantic, as they attempt to get through their workload. They might seem tired, and like they have less time or patience for small talk, or even others at all. They may seem more emotional; whether that is visible with tears or anger, or less explosive but still noticeable in their clipped tone or constant worried reactions in meetings and conversations. And they may even seem to be a little less enjoyable to be around and engage with. When you ask them if there is anything going on for them, or if they are stressed or concerned about anything, they might share that they are feeling stressed about their workload because it has just been added to, while they also have an important assessment coming up for their graduate studies they are trying to get through.

But you, in your experience, know them as a very capable worker, who is intelligent and generally does well at what they set their mind to, so you tell them as much. While there is certainly a role, and a time and place, for motivational and encouraging leadership moments, when empathy is needed, sometimes this approach on its own can miss the mark. What you *know* is that they are capable, competent, and often hit their workload out of the park. What you *know* is that they have performed well under this kind of workload before, so you *know* there is no real reason why that should not continue.

What you might not be aware of is this team member is neurodivergent and goes to great efforts already in order to manage their time, focus, and energy in their day for it to appear like they are a natural high achiever. Meanwhile, while everyone sees someone who can handle a 'little extra task' because they are so competent, they are actually experiencing the impact this extra task has on their very carefully constructed ecosystem.

The reason for the person's stress is actually more secondary; you not needing to particularly understand or even know the reasoning behind the stress is the first step in practising and displaying empathy. Acknowledgement of their experience, *regardless* of whether or not you see it that way, is what is most important for you to offer that empathetic connection. In that moment, you are not necessarily their manager, their boss, their colleague, or any other title; you are simply another human acknowledging how they are feeling. So often we attempt to skip over this part because we want to feel helpful, like we can provide a solution and a 'fix' for them, and they will start to feel better – and then everyone else around them might feel better too.

The time will come, after and then alongside this empathy, where you get to step into your leadership capacity, offer solutions, support, and anything else that might be useful for them. This part, especially as a leader, will be very important in its own time. But this part does not develop those authentic connections between you and those in your team – whether you lead them or co-work with them – as a stand-in replacement for empathy. Empathy is the acknowledgement that they are having this experience, regardless of whether you see the circumstances in the same way. Your truth, seeing things your way, can exist at the same time as this other person seeing things their way, experiencing their truth, based on their experience. What you do next with it is how you move forward, but it is important to keep that in mind as you lead: two truths can exist at once when it comes to having human experiences. How you understand things will not necessarily take away from the reality of how someone else understands and feels – often emotionally – about those same things.

Emotional Intelligence in Empathy Is More than Just Acknowledging the Experience

All of that being said, acknowledging another's experience is only the beginning of empathy, especially for a leader who will probably have further responsibilities at that point to continue to tend to. Goleman's theory of emotional intelligence continues to highlight that while cognitive intelligence (IQ) is important, emotional intelligence (EI) is equally critical for leadership success. This is especially so in areas like personal credibility, team dynamics, and organisational influence. Goleman's emotional intelligence model enforces the idea that developing these competencies can enhance performance, leadership effectiveness, and wellbeing.

Developing empathy is the same process as developing emotional intelligence; they are inherently similar practices that require you to step outside of, or aside from, your own experience or reactions just enough to acknowledge that of another person. Where empathy on its own is considered a kind way to be towards those around you and those in the topic of discussion, emotional intelligence is where the practice of empathy becomes a leadership attribute that helps others feel considered, psychologically safer, and goes further to better support the culture and longevity of the organisation in which you inhabit at that same time. In an ideal world, having a workplace or organisational culture rich with empathy should be sufficient to stoke the desire to more proactively build it. Where that fails to be sufficient, some organisations might understand better when you can convey in metrics more aligned to what translates for others.

Cultivating a culture rich with emotional intelligence intentionally can create stronger leaders; in both yourself, as well as in the case of peer leadership, where we are more likely to work alongside each other in support of not just our own success and gain, but that of our peers too. While the world and society evolve, traditional business values are becoming far less valued. They are giving way to the more valid concerns around environmental impact, economic ethics, and wealth disparity while the struggle of billions becomes louder. Genuinely emotionally intelligent leaders will naturally build more personal credibility than that of their more traditional counterparts.

An interesting cultural leadership example is Jeff Bezos. The founder of Amazon and long-standing one of the richest people in the world, if not *the* richest, has long been lauded as someone who *does business well* due to his financial success. Countless books have been written, podcast episodes recorded, interviews discussed, and even business courses created, that laud the success of Bezos, highlighting mostly, or only, the financial aspects that measure that success. It is hard to deny, when the numbers so clearly measure what is a successful business, and with Bezos at the helm, what must be by extension or cause, a successful leader.

Progressively over recent years, financial success has stopped being the predominant metric by which the worldwide audience judges a business leader's capability. Now more than ever, it is more broadly accepted that what you do with that success and how you treat others around you in order to attain that, or any, level of success is either just as important, or even more so, than how you got there in the first place. *Doing business well* at the expense of the wellbeing of those around that leader, those who are involved in helping the business to function in the way that it does, is not valued in the same way that it used to be. If anything, it is something that has the capacity to tarnish or bolster your perception as a leader, depending on how you behave with and towards others. So when it comes to being a leader who genuinely practises emotional intelligence, even if imperfectly, for the sake of how others around you feel – and not just for the profit line of the accounting statements – that can mean important things for how you yourself are perceived as a leader. When leaders have credibility beyond just how well they can *do business* and additionally more for how they treat others along the way, that can positively influence things like team dynamics. Since everyone on a team plays a role in contributing to the culture of that team, this makes way for increased – or an improvement in – organisational influence. While we know that leaders by nature of their role and the authority often given to them in that role tend to have influence in some capacity, Goleman's model of emotional intelligence suggests that emotional intelligence, when genuinely practised with empathy – that being, for the good of the experience of others, not just for the gain of the leader – can improve how successful that leader is in their role.

Emotional intelligence, just like empathy, is a competency that can be developed. Far from being just a trait that you are either born with or not, while these skills may come more naturally to some, the way that some people are naturally better at hand-eye coordination so may excel at sports with less effort, emotional intelligence builds the more it is practised. And when it is practised in a proactive, ever-evolving, continually learning and improving way by leaders, you have the chance to not only enhance your own workplace performance, but the improvements in your leadership effectiveness may actually improve yours – and others' – wellbeing and quality of life at work.

The Building Blocks of Social Intelligence

One of the common foundations of emotional intelligence, as indicated by Goleman and other researchers in this area, is social awareness. Sometimes phrased as social intelligence or social skills, this core tenet of emotional intelligence is what happens next when we are in the self-awareness and self-management practices; it is what reflects outwardly how our inner awareness begins to acknowledge those around us.

There can be some shame experienced around wanting to develop social skills as an adult. While typically seen as a skill we teach children or dogs, learning social skills as an adult tends to be put aside for the more appealing-sounding 'networking' or 'sales' skills the moment we hit employment. While these are skills that can be beneficial in business, it risks leaving 'social skills' behind. Social skills are a skill set in their own right that often fill in the gaps that skills like networking and sales cannot touch. They are different, yet are often used interchangeably to a detriment.

Beginning with self-awareness allows our social skills to develop on a foundation that is predicated on the practice of empathy. As we have previously explored, self-awareness allows you to acknowledge your own experiences. When we understand more of our own experiences, it naturally becomes easier to acknowledge that others may have their own experiences; we understand the feeling of a relationship breakdown someone else might be going through better when we have experienced our own version of separation; we understand the feeling a colleague may have of showing up to work while still grieving their deceased parent, when we too have felt that loss or grief in our own way; we can more easily acknowledge someone else feels stressed if we have acknowledged our own experiences of stress – even if the cause or circumstances are entirely different to each other. This is where we build the bridge of self-awareness into empathy, into social intelligence. We cannot *know* everything someone else is going through, feeling, or thinking, but we can acknowledge it and let that lead us to social enquiry and engagement. We build our social skills stronger on the foundation of self-learning.

As leaders, there is a considerable amount of influence you both naturally have, a given in relation to your role, as well as the capacity to develop even more of, in most cases because you have more access to opportunities to do so. Your influence in how you communicate with your team members, colleagues, managers, and peers can inform not only something as large and significant as the entire workplace culture, but also the smaller details in how a single person you interact with feels about their day or satisfaction in their own work. This influence on communication also develops into a conflict management – or resolution – style that can be done mindfully, with awareness from you as a leader, or it can be carried out a little more recklessly, without thought or consideration for the impact it might have. In order to do these things well with more of a positive impact, all of these factors – your influence, communication style, and how you navigate conflict – require you to be developing an understanding of your own needs, automatic behaviours that you lean on without awareness, and the factors that activate reactions in you.

This awareness also supports how you give and receive feedback as a leader. Part of your leadership position, whether it is employment or vocational, or your role within a system such as being a part of your family, requires you to be able to capably give feedback. There is no succinct step-by-step guide to offer that will fit exactly every interaction and dynamic; there are simply too many variables involved in order to keep it succinct and simple, from the circumstances through to the people involved. Your role as a leader when it comes to feedback is in part to learn to adapt. In part, this adaptation is required for you. Your self-awareness of what factors are influencing how you are feeling, how you are deciding, whether you have considered each perspective – or asked for other perspectives – and whether there is any kind of bias informing your feedback, including confirmation bias, and also what that bias is attempting to inform you of. Your practice of self-awareness will help you to critically assess each of these moments as they arise, so that when you do give feedback, it is with a critical awareness. That, along with any adjustments to your feedback or how you will carry it out, having taken place as a result of this awareness.

Another part of giving feedback as a leader following on from self-awareness is then interpersonal awareness; that is, the practice of emotional intelligence that helps you to engage in the kind of potentially challenging conversation with someone where they are able to receive the feedback and feel clear and even encouraged in their next steps – whether those next steps are improvement or related to any changes required. This interpersonal awareness is your awareness of how to best communicate feedback to this person, including understanding how this person uniquely best receives feedback. Clear, direct notes embolden and motivate some people with directives that are not sugarcoated; they want to be told exactly what to do, or what not to do, or how to improve. Others can feel embarrassed by that approach. Even where they desire to learn how to improve, there is a different way they thrive when receiving feedback such as this; this can be methods such as sitting down with them to workshop the problem or issue, helping them to come to those conclusions more themselves rather than the directive approach that can feel more confronting and less supportive. People grow and shrink based on various stimuli, particularly in how we communicate. As a leader, you will not always get it right in how you communicate with others and deliver feedback as needed. Sometimes you will want to avoid it entirely, potentially even avoiding it until it has become worse than the initial need for feedback in the first place, and then have to navigate that in addition to the rest. Sometimes you will rush too quickly into giving feedback, potentially before having all the information or context on hand that could refine your feedback into something more useful, even determining whether feedback is useful at all. Trust that there is always a repair process available and that you should use it willingly and liberally as a leader.

Feedback itself does not remain in a one-way direction as a leader, with the feedback only being given to others by you. An important part of first even getting to a position of leadership, and then also carrying that position out well in a way that continually looks to improve and do better, is being able to receive feedback. For many people, receiving feedback is a skill they must actively work at in order to improve upon. It can feel uncomfortable, especially when you are in a position where it is often expected that you also know what the 'next best step' is at any given moment you're called upon. It can feel uncomfortable to be reminded of the fact that, despite your position in leading your company, organisation, or team, you actually do not know everything in every moment, and that can mean mistakes and missteps, or even areas of improvement as identified by others around you. It can feel additionally uncomfortable when that feedback to you as a leader requires an adjusted approach to whole business strategy. It is not just our egos or feelings that might get bruised when we receive feedback, but it can feel bigger if it requires workload to respond and create that shift.

Leaders who are more self-aware show signs of being more open to feedback, despite these challenges, and can often respond less defensively. This can be because self-awareness helps us to catch and name our reactions better and more in real time, so that we can still get a handle on choosing how we want to respond instead. It can also be because self-awareness gives us the perspective of empathy; recognising that it might be challenging for a team member of yours to speak up, no matter how welcoming you make the environment. Self-awareness helps us as leaders to keep in mind the perspective of what is for everyone's greater good, so even if our initial reaction is to take it personally, whether or not that is warranted, it does not linger and feed into how we then respond to the situation and move forward. This allows us as leaders to be better equipped to grow – both personally and supporting the team to move forward and grow too.

When you have a team who experiences self-aware leaders who are open to and more capable of receiving feedback that can then improve everyone's experience, you get to notice the improvements in team culture that occur as a flow-on effect. Self-aware leaders who model emotional transparency and authenticity beyond just the good, easy times, and also in the face of their own room for improvement, create more psychologically safe teams because they are leading by example. They are showing you that feedback and being open to improvement is for everyone, including them, and in doing so, they create safety within teams who might otherwise fear – or in some cases, experience – repercussions simply by speaking up and suggesting something otherwise.

Defensive leaders who have not worked on this skill of receiving feedback have been known to react with volatility, which shifts the stability of any environment they exist in. This can also result in not just leaders who won't improve their behaviours, but uncertainty in their team members that can result in a higher turnover, if people don't feel as if their position is stable, or increased absenteeism and even stress leave, if team members are remaining in the volatile workplace but affected by their experiences as they attempt to navigate it.

Conflict Resolution with Emotional Intelligence

Conflict in the workplace can present in a variety of ways: competition or competing to win, disagreement or disrespect, perceived or actual injustice, malicious intent, or even, potentially more neutral, change and the management of it. Because of its volatile nature, conflict in the workplace can bring up a lot of heightened emotions and responses. In a study surveying 139 undergraduate management students (Jordan & Troth, 2002), researchers proposed that conflict itself is inherently an emotional response, because it involves perceived threats to individual goals. So when change comes sweeping in, an opposing decision is made, or a standard of respect isn't upheld, it can threaten the standing of the individual impacted. While some threats are perceived and can be ultimately superficial, others can be quite detrimental to the experience that person has in the workplace environment and also for their future.

This is where emotional intelligence in practice and in training comes in.

That same study by Jordan and Troth (2002) determined that emotional intelligence training can help to equip employees with specific self-management skills they need to engage in collaborative problem-solving, thus helping to reduce and resolve workplace conflicts. Emotional intelligence is not a fixed trait for life, so training in this area can help individuals to practise more self-awareness of what they are feeling emotionally, and manage and work on regulating those feelings so that their responses are able to be made with more choice, instead of remaining overwhelmed in the reaction.

Think back to the story about Aleesha and the director who lectured her on an hour-long phone call early on in her career. Aleesha defaulted to attempts at a collaborative solution, but didn't possess the authority to really lead any of the change. If that director had been able to recognise more of his responses and reactions in his behaviour in the moment, he might have been better able to meet her in that collaborative space, rather than remaining in the combative conflict. He might have been able to recognise where he had other stresses at play, so he could address them sooner – whether or not they were work-related or more personal in nature.

The study determined that emotional intelligence training helps to improve conflict resolution by:

- Promoting more collaboration in lieu of force or avoidance when it comes to conflict. This happens because of the developed emotional ability to recognise the needs of others while managing one's own emotions, so the individuals involved are more able and likely to seek mutually advantageous solutions, even in the event of conflict.

- Improving emotional control through management and regulation. Emotional intelligence as a skillset helps individuals to engage mindfulness to bring awareness to their emotional reactions, and then work through the dysregulation or heightened emotions they might be feeling. Not because those emotions aren't necessarily valid, but because how they respond will determine how they are able to then move forward successfully or otherwise.
- Developing the skills and normalising the culture to discuss emotions more openly and productively. When conflict is approached collaboratively, with individuals involved attempting to achieve mutual gains, this can only happen successfully if the parties involved are able to discuss and manage their own emotions. The study specifically points out that this is different to just having that initial awareness or ability to read others, which further reinforces that key next step of being able to put that awareness into useful practice.

The Thomas-Kilmann model of conflict resolution styles identifies five conflict resolution strategies based on assertiveness and cooperativeness. Those strategies are:

1. Forcing,
2. Avoiding,
3. Accommodating,
4. Compromising, and
5. Collaborating.

Initial emotional reactions to any type of conflict might have you feeling justified in forcing your way through, or worried enough to avoid it entirely or over-accommodate into further imbalance. Looking at these styles, regardless of that initial desire to just have things your way, collaboration appears to be the only version of conflict resolution that is useful in a workplace.

Collaborating doesn't mean needing to be around someone who, for example, has bullied or harassed you and should otherwise face their own consequences. Collaborating is the opportunity to make decisions and move forward in a way that benefits all parties involved, even if that resolution means that someone is let go or departs from their typical position. Sometimes it's actually more a point of what is the better approach, out of a group of strategies where none of them actually feel appealing.

With an infinite number of scenarios of workplace conflict that may justifiably require an approach different from collaboration, this same research discovered that low levels of emotional intelligence more often led to the force and avoidance approaches, with individuals reporting feeling less control over their own emotions. So perhaps by letting go of the 'control' of force or withdrawal and opening up to finding a more viable 'win-win' solution, you are actually taking back control in a more meaningful way? In any case, developing these skills of emotional intelligence only serves to open up your options available when it comes to navigating and managing workplace conflict effectively, rather than wasting precious personal and professional resources stuck in it.

Creating a Culture of Trust and Inclusion

If you want to build trust in your workplace, it doesn't come from exclusivity, keeping your cards overall close to your chest, and saving the 'rewards' for a select few in your workplace under the guise of 'inclusion' based on performance or any other metric. A study by Akram and Pervaiz (2024) found that social inclusion has the most robust, positive, and significant effect on trust across all estimated models. It goes further to state that when societies ensure equal access to resources and decision-making for all individuals, it fosters a sense of belonging, fairness, and mutual respect. And why would you want to proactively cultivate these things in your workplace? Because these are the factors that break down barriers and encourage cooperative behaviours. Not through coercion, but through collaboration – further encouraging the need to develop emotional intelligence as a required skill set, not just when dealing with conflict but to also actively create the desired workplace environment.

This collaborative approach supported by actively practising and cultivating emotional intelligence directly supports the creation of an inclusive workplace (Igboanugo et al., 2022). When employees feel like they belong and are valued, they can more actively participate. When team members feel fewer barriers to participation, that naturally leads to more actual participation in their work, in their team, towards commonly set goals. Inclusive policies, standards, and behaviours directly increase interpersonal trust levels by fundamentally affecting how individuals interact with one another and perceive their environment. If a team member perceives their environment or co-workers as threatening, at a base level it reduces their ability to contribute at no fault of their own. As explored in an article by Igboanugo et al. (2022), striving to ensure everyone has equal access to resources, opportunities, and decision-making processes within inclusive policies has the capacity to build trust in several key ways.

- Intentionally lessening the social distance between different groups, and having policies that promote environments where people from diverse backgrounds and hierarchy levels can collaborate and participate more equally, breaks down barriers that allow misperceptions about the 'other' group to thrive. When you dismantle misperception, the entire workforce and workplace benefits by allowing in what others have to offer.
- Just like we value peer networking in business, generating equitable opportunities for team members to connect and collaborate while they build social capital and networks helps to foster a strong sense of community and

reciprocity – where the creation of interdependence for help and support directly contributes to an increase in cooperative behaviours and trust. Even when we are developing these behaviours and habits in our 'own' time, they become behaviours we bring into the workplace environment. Once again, everyone benefits.
- When we shape environments with inclusive policies, the individuals experiencing those environments feel more valued, respected, and belonging within their community. When we feel like our basic needs are, or will be, fulfilled, and trust that we will be treated fairly, our willingness to engage in positive social interactions increases. Along with that increase, so does the quality of our interpersonal interactions and connections with our team members.
- Inclusive practices that empower team members from marginalised groups to have a voice confirms that collective wellbeing is more prioritised over the individual. This promotes more equal opportunity and chance to succeed, further strengthening the mutual confidence and trust amongst team members.

While any inclusion policy requires more nuance in the actual creation of it in order to achieve true equity, teams – and therefore businesses – greatly benefit when good-faith attempts and improvements are continually made in this area. Further to that, emotional intelligence as an active skill is what can make it much easier to begin to implement inclusive behaviours, policy in place or not, from leadership where it has the most cultural impact. Emotionally intelligent leaders are better at attending, listening, questioning, reflecting, learning, and displaying restrating (Igboanugo et al., 2022), opening the way for teams who are more supported to thrive and succeed. When teams collectively and team members individually thrive and succeed more in their role because the workplace culture and leadership support them to, you have yourself a high-achieving, more effective team in your business.

5 Integration

In yoga, the last pose of a physical practice is called 'savasana'; translated from Sanskrit, it literally means 'corpse pose'. This is the pose where it looks like you're doing the least – often done in a lying down position on your back, sometimes supported by bolsters or pillows, legs stretched out, arms relaxing out to the side at about a 45 degree angle, maybe with the palms facing up and fingers naturally curling. The body is invited into rest. Often mistaken for 'just a nice relaxation', some students will actually skip this part if the education isn't as prominent or normalised within that studio's culture.

What savasana really is, is an opportunity to integrate all of the information, changes, realisations, efforts, and otherwise from the practice into your new way of being. In yoga traditionally, it is actually the entire point of the practice itself. The physical asanas (poses) are preparation for the body, removing any excess energy or distractions, so that when you come to stillness, you are more able to step into it. The point isn't to master any poses – because how can you really determine what is 'mastered' if you're meeting your body and conditions exactly where they are in the given moment? The point is to explore and notice your experience, and then *practice* sitting with it. Yoga in the western world risks us forgetting this important element of the practice itself. Just like our personal development otherwise often forgets the important element of learning to *be* more of that state, rather than hustling to *do* more all the time.

The word 'yoga', derived from Sanskrit, means *to yoke* – signifying the union of body, mind, and spirit, irrespective of your spiritual beliefs. Put more secularly, it could be described as connecting your *mind, body,* and *breath*, or *being*. All this describes is the congruency between our awareness of our experience and our ability to be with that ourselves and in who we are being as we interact with the world. At least to the best of our ability.

Traditionally, leadership texts and training keep it very analytical and cognitive. But what if you were to approach this evolved understanding of leadership and mindfulness, and how emotional intelligence – something that requires the active practice of self-awareness – can not only expand your own leadership capabilities but expand your leadership impact for more beneficial outcomes, in a similar way that involves integration. This integration can involve a plan, or strategy, or how you can begin to build more mindful habits and integrate

DOI: 10.4324/9781003632771-6

practices into your team contexts. In the process of this strategy, this integration must also involve integration moments, where you are practising, quite literally, being in the practice more than *doing* it, where it becomes another box-ticking 'win', but nothing more substantial. What if this approach to integration in applying mindfulness to your life and leadership can be inspired by an ancient practice that once was exclusive to men only, and seen as a sign of strength and fortitude?

Bringing It All Together

Just like a yoga or meditation practice helps us to learn more about ourselves in those moments we sit down with ourselves, how you approach your leadership style and practice mindfully helps you to explore more of who you are. The key to mindful leadership is being open-minded and willing enough to learn about how you respond to and experience things, particularly in relation to interacting and engaging with other people. When you know enough to know who you are, you can then begin to do something intentional about it.

Finding your leadership style is a fluid act that won't necessarily end up with you fitted out in one single look for the entirety of your career. It will develop as you do. Different situations will require different approaches along the way. You'll try one thing, notice it doesn't fit you quite right, and you'll adjust. You'll make mistakes. You won't be perfect. But perfectionism is never the goal. Applying what you've learned each time, to the best of your ability, however imperfectly, will prove to be more effective than struggling for a perfect version of leadership that doesn't exist.

Here are some steps to help you remember:

Choose What Kind of Leader You Want to Be and Don't Want to Be

Choosing the kind of leader you want to be involves both creating – and then enacting – a vision, as well as reflecting on the past. Even if it's not explicitly *your* past, recognise that history can inform us of how the slippery slope to dangerous leadership styles can come from a simple desire if we don't recognise and catch it.

This is why values work is so important alongside this. Understanding our own values makes the decision-making process along the way a much simpler act. It also helps us to come back to the core tenets of what we stand for in leadership, even when things feel frustrating and we may want to cut corners just to progress things along. Values can help us catch poor decisions that require behaviour that doesn't align with what we are trying to create and cultivate. It can be the difference between a decision made with haste in mind that leads to a subsequent action that discriminates against, undermines, or otherwise harms someone else, for example, and a decision that recognises the urge for haste, but doesn't sacrifice the values of an inclusive environment for the sake of that haste. It finds a way forward that doesn't sacrifice your values just to get there.

While it won't serve you to strive for perfection, you can aim to make the best decision possible based on what you know *now*, each time that need presents. Choosing what kind of leader you want to be extends beyond just the decisions that lead to the shiny moments of leadership glory. While they can be nice and inject more positive energy or motivation into your role, you must also choose what kind of leader you want to be in conflict as well. Only focusing on an ideal of leadership that allows only room for best-case scenario outcomes, and little room for leading through challenge or undesirable scenarios does little to develop your skill in leadership. Pretending that conflict won't happen or exist simply because you are envisioning an idealistic utopia under your leadership command means you're not preparing yourself or your team to navigate a reality when, not if, it presents itself.

Be Honest with Yourself about Your Outdated Ideas of Leadership

Many of us have preconceived ideas of leadership based on what we learned or witnessed in our more formative years. This could be what someone else, such as your parents or guardians, told you perhaps. The way authority figures in our lives describe other more public leaders can shape how we view healthy or 'strong' leadership, without us even understanding why. If we don't take the time to analyse and question that respectfully for ourselves and to those who informed us, we don't actually learn how to discern how we perceive leadership. We don't learn how to discern whether a leader's actions are aligning with what they say, or to question ideologies that ultimately present in leadership.

Our brain's confirmation bias risks us just looking for similarities in that version of 'strong' leadership in others we meet along the way, and then in ourselves, without noticing if it's actually true to what we have in mind for our own style of leadership. Critical thinking through the confirmation bias is an important skill to continue beyond your schooling, applying it in all aspects of life in relation to how you perceive the world and make decisions. Not from the perspective of living only in a lack of trust, but from the perspective of leading yourself and your mind first. Self-leadership is an underrated and under-discussed area of leadership, but I would argue a presence, or lack of, self-leadership is where all other leadership either stems from or fails from.

Explore Mindfulness Curiously and with an Open Mind

Part of being a leader requires a certain level of open-mindedness. Do you need to be open to absolutely everything, all of the time, throwing away your own ability to discern? No, but an ability *and willingness* to always be learning is the important part. And that includes trying things a little differently than what traditional leadership models may have taught you, based on new information. Our understanding of human nature, psychology, and the real or fabricated impacts of wellbeing are ever-evolving, and like all science, ever-continuing.

This means that just because your mentor – in real life or perhaps one that you have up on a pedestal – didn't do things a certain way, doesn't mean that we haven't learned something new in these areas that would be useful for you to try and apply. All entrepreneurs know that you must be innovative and sometimes have to try something different in order to stand out, succeed, or progress forward. Whatever your position of leadership, whether that is as a business owner or internally for an organisation, it is almost a requirement that you approach how you learn and develop your leadership with the same philosophy.

Be willing to try different things, with different results and levels of personal effectiveness. Trust that it's not a failing if you learn that something doesn't work as well for you, or for any members of your team. Treat it a bit like an experiment, founded in ever-developing research and knowledge. You are a scientist in your own right.

Move Your Self-Awareness into Self-Management

You can be the most self-aware person in the world, and yet if you choose not to do anything with that information, it becomes just that: information. Self-awareness and self-management go hand in hand in this way. Self-awareness is how you determine how you then manage what you need to within or around yourself. Self-management relies on this information to function and make the most informed decisions or actions it can in support of yourself and your external environment, in any given moment. Neither is a permanent state; rather, they are active, living, breathing practices and experiences that may require different approaches or have different needs from time to time. Nor is either state intended to reach any form of perfectionism or competitiveness, whether that competition is with yourself or others. See it simply as the gathering of information, and then a plan to support yourself personally and within your world with that information.

As you can imagine, this takes active work and attention. It also requires self-compassion and grace. This is not another competition with yourself or mental load onto your list of things to do. Treat this as more of a way of being: a balance between self-care and self-alignment. Sometimes it will feel like more challenging work, and other times it will feel more like a relief for your whole system, depending on the season you are in.

You Never Know the Full Impact You Can Have as a Leader

Leadership isn't an exercise in seeking glory and notoriety. Many of the more public examples we may see of leadership are placed on a pedestal, and while having examples of what we should or shouldn't do is helpful for us to learn, the goal for you shouldn't be for the fame of it. Let your leadership be for the impact, and the recognition often follows. Having said that, no matter how much feedback you receive, we can never really know the full impact we have as a leader. How you communicate is going to lead the way in determining this impact. When your self-awareness develops into your self-management habits and practices, you can then explore how that determines your communication style and tone.

There's no particular 'right' way of communicating, in the sense that it must be authentic to you, including any needs you have. The Flourishing model in positive psychology sometimes references the ability to socialise and make eye contact as a 'good' measure of someone flourishing in their life. While it's a useful basis to begin with, if we apply this version of flourishing indicators to people who, for example, are on the autism spectrum and experience eye contact as uncomfortable, we risk determining them as more 'languishing' – the opposite of flourishing – if they cannot meet that metric. This applies to how you communicate too. There can be more than one truth around communication, even when it comes to leadership positions. It can be true that it is most useful for you to be aware of your tone or other emotions that might be impacting how you communicate with others around you, just like it's useful for you to have open dialogue with your team members to understand their communication style and preference as well. *And* it can be equally as true for you to struggle with certain conventional communication norms and 'rules', and them not being your natural way of being and thriving, if you are neurodivergent. This doesn't make you wrong or bad at communication. It is simply information that can inform the dynamic. Another big part of being a leader is setting an example and modelling ways of being and approaches to our leadership. This could be one of those examples you set by how you approach this.

Be Really Clear about What You Stand for and the Culture You're Creating

The natural follow-on from your impact as a leader is your active cultivation of the culture you are overseeing. Being really clear in what you stand for – your values and subsequent actions, communication norms and allowances you set, the lot – helps you to determine the culture you're creating. This goes the same for being clear in what you don't stand for – misaligned values and subsequent actions, harmful communication styles, what behaviour you let slide in others. Being clear in what you stand for and how each action either supports or negates the creation of that within the environment you and your team exist in is the mark of a leader. It's important to consider what mark you want to leave on the experience of those around you, not just how much money you've made the organisation.

Repeat, as Necessary

We don't reach a stage in life, just because we're no longer growing physically, that we're no longer growing in any other way. Coming back to the basics and repeating as necessary isn't a mark of failure in yourself or you as a leader. Nor is it a mark of mental or emotional weakness. It's simply a reality. Each of us will continue to make a variety of mistakes as we continue in our lives, despite our best efforts. Our practices and needs will change and evolve, or even devolve. What's effective for us today may not have the same effect next week. We practise meeting ourselves where we are at, each time, and go from there.

The Leadership Toolkit for Modern Challenges

Get Comfortable with Uncomfortable Conversations

You don't have to love them, and you can always call time – particularly if you or another person feels unsafe. But learning to lean into discomfort (not dysregulation or lack of safety) is an important tool in your toolkit for navigating life and leadership. This helps you to not avoid important conversations, but also stay more open to curiosity so you can lead them, holding space for others' discomfort that may show up, and get to the heart of the matter.

Get Used to Feedback, Even if You Disagree

Actually seek out feedback, periodically and without an air of co-dependency that suggests you *need* it from others in order to go on functioning. But feedback helps you to both understand others and how they perceive the world, as well as yourself as you navigate your responses to it. Even if you disagree and are justified in that, it brings you back to getting comfortable with navigating uncomfortable conversations as you explore that feedback with yourself and even the person who gave it. Feedback is a useful barometer check for whether your intended leadership is having the appropriate effect, or where there is misunderstanding between your message and how it's received.

Be Willing to Take Advice from Those You Trust, but You Don't Need to Take Advice from Everyone

Being a lifelong learner doesn't mean you don't know anything or can't lead yourself. So while it's important to be willing to take advice from a select, key few people you trust have your best interests at heart, your discernment can still be functioning alive and well. You can respect someone and what they've offered, and still determine – with thought, reflection and mindfulness – that it doesn't fit you best. This is how we learn.

Make Mindfulness a Habit

Mindfulness won't happen on its own. Nor will it happen with a wish and a prayer. Do enough work to make it a habit, and over time it will become easier and more a part of your way of *being*. Start simple – we don't need to build it all at once. Let yourself stack each practice little by little for more sustainability.

Don't Assume You'll Get it Right 100% of the Time

Be willing to recognise you'll make mistakes. This, too, is a part of how we learn. We're not aiming to get it wrong, ever, but it's important to keep in mind that you won't always get leadership in any sense of the word or role right 100% of the time. Keep this in mind: A lot of the time, how you repair will be even more impactful.

Take on Professional Development in Leadership like it's Your Job – and Be Willing to Adapt What You Know Based on New Things You Learn or Updates in Research

Wellbeing science and how we understand it is an evolving and growing field. Normalise updating your leadership style and practice based on updated research, or your own updated understanding of how you or others work. Leaders evolve; they don't remain stagnant.

Gather Metrics in Leadership Success beyond Financial

Some countries are beginning to explore the marker of a 'healthy' country beyond just what their Gross Domestic Product (GDP) is measured at, and including measures of wellbeing levels to help them understand a truer state of their people. Approach your leadership success in the same way. In the material world we exist in, financial measures are important in order to continue to do the work we are doing, but you can use this opportunity to lead the way in how you leave your leadership mark in the areas you exist in, and measure beyond the financial metrics into metrics that measure experience.

Your Next Steps as a Leader

Leadership requires many layers of professional development beyond just the technical skill or industry expertise. Add in that it involves other humans, their unique minds and experiences, and interpersonal dynamics, all while often in stressful work environments, and it is a complex area. The complex needs of leadership are in an era where it requires an evolution. Long have so-called 'soft skills' like mindfulness, emotional intelligence, and practices of presence directly related to the workplace been relegated consistently to the bottom of the list of priorities, but long enough have we now known just how beneficial these very skills are to the people involved, as well as the health of the business itself.

Learning these skills isn't a one-and-done method. Your understanding of yourself as you personally evolve and change over the course of your life and career, and the experiences you have along the way, will naturally shift your relationship to some of these practices or the people around you from time to time. This is why we approach this as a *practice*.

When much of life and work can feel like a competition as we strive for perfectionism and being 'the best' in our field, mindfulness in how you lead requires something else: a humility and dedication, even in the moments your awareness of it wanes.

Your best next step is to set up a plan. It doesn't need to be comprehensive and overwhelmingly take over everything else you already have in place. Even when there is enthusiasm for such a plan, many people risk having the overall goal or outcome as the plan itself. Instead, narrow it down, break it up further into singular pieces; choose something that you can start with right now.

Is it scheduling a time on your calendar, or a reminder on your phone to introduce one simple new practice (even if you're habit-stacking while you're doing something else)?

Is it having a conversation with someone else to ask for their participation?

Is it setting up a feedback system with your team so you can start to understand what they're experiencing most, which might help you focus your direction?

Is it engaging in support if you feel overwhelmed?

Pick one thing that takes you to that next natural step. We often want to be able to see the entire pathway ahead of us before we begin, when realistically all we need is to be able to see just that next step, which may be the catalyst to you opening up your view and being able to see further, understand, or comprehend more fully from there.

Pick one thing, begin to implement it, and then start to ask questions. Lead yourself into this process, whether you feel excited or your excitement has a half-life by the time you begin. Nothing happens until you start, and that includes within your team too. When you lead yourself, you are leading them by example. This is how we learn, grow, and innovate. This is the fundamental requirement of our role as a leader.

References

Akram, S., & Pervaiz, Z. (2024). The role of institutions and social inclusion in trust building. *Quality & Quantity*, *58*(4), 3887–3903. https://doi.org/10.1007/s11135-024-01851-8

Alkoby, A., Pliskin, R., Halpern, E., & Levit-Binnun, N. (2018). An eight-week mindfulness-based stress reduction (MBSR) workshop increases regulatory choice flexibility. *Emotion*, *19*, 593–604.

Awan, U., Sufyan, M., Ameer, I., Shamim, S., Akhtar, P., & Zia, N. U. (2024). Mindfulness and creative process engagement: The mediating role of workplace relational systems. *Journal of Managerial Psychology*, *39*(3), 241–263. https://doi.org/10.1108/JMP-04-2022-0196

Baer, R. A. (2011). Measuring mindfulness. Contemporary Buddhism, 12, 241–261

Bartlett, L., Martin, A., Neil, A. L., Memish, K., Otahal, P., Kilpatrick, M., & Sanderson, K. (2019). A systematic review and meta-analysis of workplace mindfulness training randomized controlled trials. *Journal of Occupational Health Psychology*, *24*(1), 108–126. https://doi.org/10.1037/ocp0000146

Baumeister, R. F., Bratslavsky, E., Finkenauer, C., & Vohs, K. D. (2001). Bad is stronger than good. *Review of General Psychology*, *5*(4), 323–370. https://doi.org/10.1037/1089-2680.5.4.323

Brewer, J. (2014). Mindfulness in the military. *American Journal of Psychiatry*, *171*(8), 803–806. https://doi.org/10.1176/appi.ajp.2014.14040501

Brown, B. (2018). *Dare to lead: Brave work. Tough conversations. Whole hearts.* Random House.

Cherniss, C., Extein, M., Goleman, D., & Weissberg, R. P. (2006). Emotional intelligence: What does the research really indicate? *Educational Psychologist*, *41*(4), 239–245. https://doi.org/10.1207/s15326985ep4104_4

Choi, E., Farb, N., Pogrebtsova, E., Gruman, J., & Grossmann, I. (2021). What do people mean when they talk about mindfulness? *Clinical Psychology Review*, *89*, 102085. https://doi.org/10.1016/j.cpr.2021.102085

Copeland, M. K. (2014). *The Emerging Significance of Values Based Leadership: A Literature Review. 8.*

Desbordes, G., Negi, L. T., Pace, T. W. W., Wallace, B. A., Raison, C. L., & Schwartz, E. L. (2012). Effects of mindful-attention and compassion meditation training on amygdala response to emotional stimuli in an ordinary, non-meditative state. *Frontiers in Human Neuroscience*, *6*. https://doi.org/10.3389/fnhum.2012.00292

Dixon, M. L., Thiruchselvam, R., Todd, R., & Christoff, K. (2017). Emotion and the prefrontal cortex: An integrative review. *Psychological Bulletin*, *143*(10), 1033–1081. https://doi.org/10.1037/bul0000096

Eurich, T. (2018). *What self-awareness really is (and how to cultivate it)*. Harvard Business Review. https://membership.amavic.com.au/files/What%20self-awareness%20is%20and%20how%20to%20cultivate%20it_HBR_2018.pdf

Fundação Getulio Vargas (Brazil), Université de Bordeaux (France), Dias, M. D. O., Pan, J., Vieira, P., & Pereira, L. J. D. (2022). From Plato to e-Leaders: The evolution of leadership theories and styles. *Journal of Economics and Business*, *5*(2). https://doi.org/10.31014/aior.1992.05.02.420

Goleman, D., & Cherniss, C. (2024). Optimal Leadership and Emotional Inteligence. Leader to Leader, 2024(113), 7–12. https://doi org /10.1002/ltl .20813

Harris, D. J., Vine, S. J., & Wilson, M. R. (2017). Neurocognitive mechanisms of the flow state. In *Progress in brain research* (Vol. 234, pp. 221–243). Elsevier. https://doi.org/10.1016/bs.pbr.2017.06.012

Hölzel, B. K., Carmody, J., Vangel, M., Congleton, C., Yerramsetti, S. M., Gard, T., & Lazar, S. W. (2011). Mindfulness practice leads to increases in regional brain gray matter density. *Psychiatry Research: Neuroimaging*, *191*(1), 36–43. https://doi.org/10.1016/j.pscychresns.2010.08.006

Hülsheger, U. R., Alberts, H. J. E. M., Feinholdt, A., & Lang, J. W. B. (2013). Benefits of mindfulness at work: The role of mindfulness in emotion regulation, emotional exhaustion, and job satisfaction. *Journal of Applied Psychology*, *98*(2), 310–325. https://doi.org/10.1037/a0031313

Igboanugo, S., Yang, J., & Bigelow, P. (2022). Building a framework for an inclusive workplace culture: The Diversio Diversity and Inclusion Survey. *The International Journal of Information, Diversity, & Inclusion*, *6*(3), 52–67. https://www.jstor.org/stable/48700868

Jordan, P. J., & Troth, A. C. (2002). Emotional intelligence and conflict resolution: Implications for human resource development. *Advances in Developing Human Resources*, *4*(1), 62–79. https://doi.org/10.1177/1523422302004001005

Kiker, D. S., & Callahan, J. S. (2019). *Exploring the Boundaries of Servant Leadership: A Meta-Analysis of the Main and Moderating Effects of Servant Leadership on Behavioral and Affective Outcomes.* (2).

Krén, H., & Séllei, B. (2020). The role of emotional intelligence in organizational performance. *Periodica Polytechnica Social and Management Sciences*, *29*(1), 1–9. https://doi.org/10.3311/PPso.15879

Nagoski, A. (2025). *Burnout Prevention for Conductors and Their Choirs. 62*(3*Military Psychology*, *36*(6), 661–671. https://doi.org/10.1080/08995605.2023.2250709

Park, B. J., Tsunetsugu, Y., Kasetani, T., Kagawa, T., & Miyazaki, Y. (2010). The physiological effects of Shinrin-yoku (taking in the forest atmosphere or forest bathing): Evidence from field experiments in 24 forests across Japan. *Environmental Health and Preventive Medicine*, *15*(1), 18–26. https://doi.org/10.1007/s12199-009-0086-9

Pedler, M. (2011). Leadership, risk and the imposter syndrome. *Action Learning: Research and Practice*, *8*(2), 89–91. https://doi.org/10.1080/14767333.2011.581016

Polizzi, C. P., Wachen, J. S., Straud, C. L., Mintz, J., Baier, A. L., Dondanville, K. A., Young-McCaughan, S., Litz, B. T., Yarvis, J. S., Peterson, A. L., Resick, P. A., & for the STRONG STAR Consortium. (2024). Exploring the associations of emotion regulation and trait resilience with the efficacy of cognitive processing therapy for active duty military personnel with PTSD. *Cognitive Therapy and Research*, *48*(4), 676–686. https://doi.org/10.1007/s10608-023-10457-7

Rocco, M. L., & Davis, K. R. (2024). Expanding the boundaries of leadership development: Propositions for leadership educators. *New Directions for Student Leadership*, *2024*(183), 51–58. https://doi.org/10.1002/yd.20623

Stanley, D. (2008). Congruent leadership: Values in action. *Journal of Nursing Management*, *16*(5), 519–524. https://doi.org/10.1111/j.1365-2834.2008.00895.x

Van Agteren, J., Iasiello, M., Lo, L., Bartholomaeus, J., Kopsaftis, Z., Carey, M., & Kyrios, M. (2021). A systematic review and meta-analysis of psychological interventions to improve mental wellbeing. *Nature Human Behaviour*, *5*(5), 631–652. https://doi.org/10.1038/s41562-021-01093-w

Zeidan, F., Johnson, S. K., Diamond, B. J., David, Z., & Goolkasian, P. (2010). Mindfulness meditation improves cognition: Evidence of brief mental training. *Consciousness and Cognition*, *19*(2), 597–605. https://doi.org/10.1016/j.concog.2010.03.014

Zhao, L., & Huang, H. (2025). The double-edged sword effects of leader perfectionism on employees' job performance: The moderating role of self-efficacy. *Frontiers in Psychology*, *16*, 1412064. https://doi.org/10.3389/fpsyg.2025.1412064

Žydžiūnaitė, V. (2018). Leadership Values and Values Based Leadership: What is the Main Focus? *Applied Research In Health And Social Sciences: Interface And Interaction*, *15*(1), 43–58. https://doi.org/10.2478/arhss-2018-0005

Index

www.ingramcontent.com/pod-product-compliance
Ingram Content Group UK Ltd.
Pitfield, Milton Keynes, MK11 3LW, UK
UKHW022018180926
475701UK00005B/914